KENNETH

FIDGET

GOLDSMITH

Coach House Books

CANADIAN CATALOGUING IN PUBLICATION DATA

Goldsmith, Kenneth
        Fidget

Poems.
ISBN 1 55245 076 7

1. Title.

PS3557.O3856F53 2000   811'.54   C00-930538-6

In a *dérive*, one or more persons during a certain period drop their usual motives for movement and action, their relations, their work and leisure activities, and let themselves be drawn by the attractions or the terrain and the encounters they find there.

— Guy Debord

... to fidget with points of view leads always to new beginnings and incessant new beginnings lead to sterility.

—Wallace Stevens, in a letter to William Carlos Williams, 1918

10:00

Eyelids open. Tongue runs across upper lip moving from left side of mouth to right following arc of lip. Swallow. Jaws clench. Grind. Stretch. Swallow. Head lifts. Bent right arm brushes pillow into back of head. Arm straightens. Counterclockwise twist thrusts elbow toward ceiling. Tongue leaves interior of mouth, passing through teeth. Tongue slides back into mouth. Palm corkscrews. Thumb stretches. Forefingers wrap. Clench. Elbow bends. Thumb moves toward shoulder. Joint of thumb meets biceps. Elbow turns upward as knuckles of fist jam neck. Right hand clenches. Thumb rubs knuckles. Fist to right shoulder. Right elbow thrusts. Knuckles touch side of neck. Hands unfurl. Backs of hands press against flat of neck. Heels of hands push into jaw. Elbows raise. Fingers wrap around neck. Thumbs tuck. Hands move toward jaw. Cover ears. Tips of fingers graze side of head. Hairs tickle tips as they pass. Thumbs trail behind fingers. Arms extend. Fingers unfurl. Shoulder stretches. Arms out. Legs bend at knees. Pelvis thrusts right. Left knee drops to bed. Right knee drops to bed. Left leg extends. Right hand grabs. Elbow moves toward nose. Touches. Fingers open. Air from lungs expelled through nose. Thumb and forefinger pinch, wiping mucus from lip. Mucus pools in right nostril. Wipes. Index finger blocks right nostril. Exhale. Mucus out right nostril. Elbow extends. Fingers open. Forefinger caresses outside of thumb.

Breathe. Right hand twists. Right foot propels body forward. Right hip stretches. Right knee drops, almost touching bed. Muscles in right thigh and left buttocks stretch. Mucus drawn from nose into back of throat. Tongue gathers saliva and mucus. Swallow. Right hand moves to nose. Right thumb covers nostril. Exhale. Expel. Right index finger moves to forehead near top of hairline. Itches four times. Finger moves from hairline to eyebrow. Body contracts into fetal position. Right arm rests between knees. Knees curve as body flips right. Left hand slides beneath right ear. Elbow bends. Mucus pulled from nose to throat. Floods back of mouth. Gathers in pouch of right cheek. Tongue coats top row of teeth in mucus. Pushes to back of mouth. Swallow. Tongue produces watery saliva. Curls. Swallow. Neck muscles tighten. Inhale. Air pins tongue to teeth. Swallow. Watery saliva dissolves mucus. Right hand to face. Pinkie rubs eye. Index finger massages right eyebrow. Middle finger digs into left eye. Thrusts. Hands between legs. Stretch. Body on side. Yawn. Stretch. Knees bend. Toes arch. Teeth clench. Jaw closes. Pelvis thrusts. Bottom teeth hit upper. Left temple tightens. Hand raises. Moves to back. Drops to buttocks. Fingernails scratch. Index finger extends into crack of buttocks and probes anus. Scratches once, twice, three times. Strong pressure applied by fingertip. Finger glides over coccyx and out of buttocks.

Arm extends. Yawn. Elbow bends. Hand drops. Forefinger moves to nostril. Enters. Tip of finger probes ridges inside nostril. Shape of left nostril conforms to shape of finger. Shape of finger conforms to shape of left nostril. Finger removes caked mucus from nostril. Wipes. Arms lock behind head. Back arches. Pelvis thrusts. Stretches. Stomach expands. Exhale. Yawn. Right leg lifts. Dangles. Left leg arcs. Hands move behind head. Left arm stretches. Knees crash. Bend. Right knee falls to bed. Flattens. Left leg waves. Bends. Straightens. Swallow. Eyes lips. Mouth forms round o of swallow. Eyes nose. Squints. Nose doubles. Closes. Views nose profile to left. Vision blocked by shadow. Closes. Eyes profile nose to right. Open. Eyebrows lift. Forehead muscles flex. Eyes right. Eyes down. Eyes profile nose. Eyes left. Eyes up. Yawn. Torso flexes. Left leg stretches. Relaxes. Pelvis thrusts. Left hand to face. Catches saliva. Tongue licks upper lip left to right. Head props on pillow. Right leg bends. Back flat. Left leg bends. Left toes dig into underside of right knee. Right heel brushes hairs of left leg. Right side of knee touches ground. Mucus pulled into throat. Left leg touches bed. Motion in left thigh. Blood in leg. Subsides. Belly fills. Lungs expand. Belly falls. Belly rises. Belly falls. Belly rises from navel. Belly falls. Belly rises. Belly falls. Right leg moves away. Left leg scrapes ankle. Yawn. Knees extend. Stretch starts at upper ribcage.

Ends at temple. Flips right. Bends. Arches. Right knee moves to edge of bed. Right foot stretches. Touches floor. Tip of big toe hits. Second toe, third toe, fourth toe, pinkie toe touch. Knees forward. Ball of foot touches. Left leg propels body. Back flat on bed. Left hand thrusts body into erect position. Straightens from torso. Upright. Right heel touches ground. Right foot supports body weight. Left leg leaves bed. Knees straighten. Left foot hits ground. Eyes ahead. Body turns right. Right foot swings right. Left foot follows. Left foot steps. Begins at ball. Ends at heel. Step. Step. Right heel hits. Weight on ball. Left foot raises. Weight shifts right. Right foot leaves ground. Steps forward. Heel hits. Followed by ball. Knees bend. Right foot extends. Mucus pulled into back of throat. Right foot steps. Step. Step. Step. Step. Step. Left hand moves away. Fingers open. Hand moves to body. Turns right. Feet forward. Step. Pinches back. Left hand grasps. Arm moves behind. Sidesteps left. Knees bend. Buttocks drop. Elbow pushes. Right hand corkscrews, led by tip of right middle finger. Fist in front of body. Right hand scratches right calf. Right thumb and forefinger pinch.

11:00

Thumb and forefinger grasp. Pull toward floor. Right hand moves palm upward. Back of hand holds as thumb and forefingers grab. Forefinger moves away. Thumb and middle finger grasp. Palm of hand receives. Thumb and middle finger grasp. Palm of hand opens. Holds bottom side of thumb. Left hand releases and moves to top. Hand retreats. Right hand lifts. Left hand grabs. Turns over. Tips of left fingers dig into scalp. Left hand, grasping with left thumb and two fingers, thrust into palm. Fingers grasp as body swings left. Head turns. Left thumb, middle and forefinger grab. Left finger lifts and releases. Body moves, arching forward. Knees straighten. Body erect. Step right. Step left foot. Step right foot. Step left foot. Hips swing to right. Right hand grasps, moving away from body. Using thumb and forefinger, muscles in thumb twist counterclockwise. Body weight on left foot. Right foot poised away from body. Ball of foot touches ground. Heel raises. Thumb and forefinger of right hand twist clockwise. Hand outstretches. From underneath, forefingers wrap. Right arm lifts and moves to top. Hand releases. Palms down. Elbows out. Twisting hand pushes thumb and forefinger left forcing body left. Finger and thumb move to right. Hand returns to side. Body turns. Walks. Left foot. Head raises. Walk. Forward. Forward. Forward. Bend at knees. Forward. Right foot. Left foot. Right foot. Stop. Left hand tucks at pubic area.

Extracts testicles and penis using thumb and forefinger. Left hand grasps penis. Pelvis pushes on bladder, releasing urine. Stream emerges from within buttocks. Stomach and buttocks push outward. Stream of urine increases. Buttocks push. Sphincter tightens. Buttocks tighten. Thumb and forefinger shake penis. Thumb pulls. Left hand reaches. Tip of forefinger and index finger extend to grasp as body sways to left. Feet pigeon-toed. Move to left. Hand raises to hairline and pushes hair. Arm raises above head. Four fingers comb hair away from hairline toward back of head. Eyes see face. Mouth moves. Small bits of saliva cling to inside of lips. Swallow. Lips form words. Teeth mechanically open as tongue slides in and out. Tip of tongue hits tip of teeth. Facial muscles displace ears and temples. Facial muscles relax. Swallow. Tongue moistens upper lip. Nose wrinkles. Space between eyebrows affected by speech. Blink. Residual blink in left eye. Back of jaw forces ears to quiver. Small movements from inner ear. Jaw thrusts bit of inner ear. Right hand raises. Digs between tear duct and nose. Caresses tear duct. Left hand grasps. Forefinger and middle finger squeeze. Left hand grabs. Moves close to right hand. Thumb and forefinger apply pressure. Left hand covers. Turns counterclockwise. Right arm swings back and forth. Mouth opens. Right hand enters mouth. Left cheek puffs. Teeth cool. Tongue sweats. Right hand fists. Teeth grind back and forth. Noise in ears. Mouth gathers saliva. Lips purse and expel. Upper teeth comb lower lip. Hand opens. Shifts to right. Arm moves back and forth. Gum jams lips. Cheek inflates. Tongue expels. Sucks to back of mouth. Hand twists around back of teeth. Tongue gathers. Expels. Left hand twists clockwise, driven by thumb and forefinger. Hand drops. Moves to face. Expels water. Right hand cups. Left hand cups. Hands turn around each other. Right hand caresses left. Cupped hands to face. Face to cupped hands. Massages. Fingers dig into tear ducts. Small areas on face and broad areas on neck caressed by hands. Hands move away from body, massaging each other. Hands cup. Bring to face. Hands squeeze neck muscles. Apply pressure behind ears. Forefingers dig. Caress eyebrows. Hands move away from body. Arms outstretch. Hands grip. Twist. Neck bows right. Pressure on forehead, face and neck. Right hand grips. Meets left. Left hand grips. Meets right. Fingers caress opposite hand. Right finger moves to nose, then to hairline. Smooth hair. Body turns left. Drops down. Step one. Step two. Step three. Step four. Ball of right foot hits. Meets eye. Rubs repeatedly. Step. Step. Step. Step. Step. Step. Back. Left hand reaches with index finger. Thumb flicks. Hand returns to side. Right hand dangles from arm forty-five degrees. Arm twists. Left hand parallels. Arm outstretches. Grasps. Fingers pass to right hand.

Left hand grasps. Arm moves away from body. Left hand scratches right forearm. Right-hand fingers spread. Close. Body pivots. Walks straight. Hand releases. Body reverses. Right hand extends. Body thrusts forward. Hands form circular shape. Grasp. Body moves forward. Hand releases. Right hand pushes away. Grasps. Body rises. Walks straight. Fingernails jam. Right arm lifts. Outstretches. Thumb, forefinger and middle finger join. Fist clenches. Arm drops two hundred twenty degrees then reverses forty degrees. Repeats three times. Fist unclenches. Right middle finger overlaps right index finger. Grasps. Heel of hand applies pressure. Right thumb controls. Right elbow tips. Right hand falls. Elbow lowers. Right arm swings across body. Extends outward. Three fingers form star. Grasp. Raise from biceps. Small circular motion repeats several times. Wrist twists. Fingers separate. Elbow tucks close to body. Left hand reaches and grasps circular formation. Body turns. Backs up. Walks. Left foot. Right foot. Left foot. Body hunches. Swings. Elbow extends. Forms ninety-degree angle with body. Shoulder lifts above elbow. Arm flips. Fingers release. Left. Right. Feet crash together. Knees bend in squatting position. Weight on balls of feet. Left hand reaches between legs and grasps. Body lifts. Foot slides left. Body bends. Reels backwards. Left hand releases. Elbow pulls arm back to body. Step. Step. Step. Step.

Left hand perpendicular to body. Middle finger extends. Presses outward. Fingers curl. Hand drops. Left foot. Right foot. Head raises. Right foot. Left foot. Hand grasps arm. Buttocks lower. Body swings. Moves forward. Hunches over. Hand, palm up, extends. Arms close to body. Falls six inches. Hands grasp. Left hand touches thumb. Four fingers relax. Elbow raises. Hand moves away. Fingers slide underneath. Press away. Elbow returns to arm. Left fingers scratch forehead. Top of finger wipes bottom of nose. Middle finger drops fifteen degrees. Fingers slightly arch. Middle finger thrusts. Arm follows finger. Springs from wrist. Hand lies flat. Palms down. Left hand rests on lap. Finger pushes up and down. Right thumb clicks. Hands return to lap. Yawn. Stomach growls. Left hand drags. Index finger points. Thumb hits. Once. Twice. Twice quickly. Pinkie and forefinger press. Hand returns to lap. Right palm presses. Hand grasps. Elbow extends. Elbow returns. Elbow extends. Thumb and forefinger flick. Thumb and middle finger rotate. Hand opens. Clenches. Right wrist turns counterclockwise. Applies pressure to upper surface of thumb. Grasps. Bends at wrist. Moves toward mouth. Lips part. Purse. Hand tips. Inhale. Tongue and saliva roll in mouth. Swallow. Tongue emerges through teeth and lips. Tongue lies on lower lip. Teeth click tongue. Lower jaw drops from upper. Flesh folds beneath chin. Repeats.

Upper lip sucks. Rubs against bottom. Swallow. Saliva gathers under tongue. Teeth tuck inside jaw. Gather saliva. Swallow. Left hand, grasping with three fingers, moves toward mouth. Swallow. Arm drops. Arm lifts. Swallow. Arm drops. Swallow. Arm lifts. Arm drops. Eyes move to left. Left hand hits. Arm lifts. Swallow. Arm drops. Right leg crosses left.

12:00

Breathe while grasping. Elbow out. Hand down. Pour coffee. Elbow down. Hand up. Back on back. Hands on arms of chair slide back. Arm stretches. Grasps milk. Elbow down. Elbow up. Elbow down. Arms stretches. Elbow down. Elbow on chair. Chair on elbow. Hand on hand. Legs cross. Back on back of chair. Legs touch legs. Arms parallel arms of chair. Hands grasp end of arms. Legs push back. Feet flat on ground. Elbow on arm. Arms out. Cup to mouth. Swallow. Cup put down. Cup to mouth. Swallow. Cup put down. Teeth outside mouth. Leg lifts. Legs stretch on legs ninety degrees. Grasp paper towels. Slide to front. Left hand grasps right. Pull away from left. Left hand stretches. Fold. Left thumb and forefinger crease. Thumbs crease. Forefingers over tips of thumbs. Thumbs and forefingers crease. Hands parallel. Tips of fingers touch thumbs on top of towel. Bring to nose. Press. Expel mucus. Exhale through nose. Right hand grasps. Rubs left nostril. Rubs right hand. Transfers to left hand. Drops on table. Fists to table. Legs cross. Right hand grasps coffee cup. Brings to mouth. Tips cup. Coffee spills into mouth. Swallow. Right hand brings coffee cup to table. Right hand grasps coffee cup. Breathe from stomach. Breathe from top of lungs. Exhale. Stomach fills with air. Exhale. Exhale. Eyes close. Pressure on eyeballs. Eyes open. Right hand grasps coffee cup with thumb, forefinger and index finger. Muscles tighten in arm.

Coffee cup to lips. Tilt. Coffee swallowed and cup placed on table. Coffee cup to lips. Coffee swallowed. Cup placed on table. Draw mucus. Swallow. Peristalsis. Cup to mouth. Coffee flows between teeth and gum inside cheek. Tip of tongue caresses inside of cheek. Tongue probes gully where cheek meets gum. Tongue muscles stretch, flex, and strain. Tongue runs along canal in front of teeth. Elbows lean against arms. Bones exact pressure. Cup to mouth. Head tilts back. Lips open. Hands outstretch and meet in front of body. Fingers clasp. Gully forms where fingers meet fingers. Forefinger of left hand in gully of forefinger and middle finger of right. Middle finger of left hand in gully of middle finger and ring finger of right. Ring finger of left hand in gully of ring finger and pinkie of right. Pinkie of left hand leans on flesh of right. Thumbs cross. Thumb of left hand in gully of thumb and forefinger of right. Bottom knuckles rub against right index finger. Thumb moves to gully of right thumb and forefinger. Thumb probes. Left thumb pushes skin of right thumb and forefinger. Configuration disperses. Left finger rubs bottom of left nostril. Left hand brings cup to lips. Tilts. Swallow. Arm extends. Tongue moves to left side of mouth and nudges space between upper and lower palate. Tongue slides across upper rim of teeth, probing crevices. Tongue moves to back of mouth. Tongue moves forward and examines front molars.

Tip of tongue slides over sharp tip of canine tooth. Slips to smooth back of tooth. Tongue slides up back of tooth, probing place where tooth and gum meet. Tongue bends at center. Circumscribes molar. Falls over adjacent molar toward back of mouth, dropping into next molar. Tongue explores crevice in middle of tooth. Aided by saliva, tongue moves to next tooth. Tip of tongue touches last molar. Mouth slightly opens. Tongue caresses smooth upper gum in back of mouth, following line where gum meets teeth. Moves to front of mouth. Surface rests against interior of fang. Hand grasps cup. Brings to lips. Head tilts back. Coffee pours into mouth. Swallow. Hand returns cup to table. Hands clutch. Fingers interlace. Jaw thrusts flat surface of tongue. Probes smooth exterior of left upper fang. Tip of tongue pushes upper lip. Tongue moves to exterior surface of left molar. Pulls jaw on right side. Veins on right side of neck bulge. Tongue runs across upper row of teeth. Pulls back and massages bottom molar on biting surface. Hand grasps cup. Brings to mouth. Head tilts back. Swallow. Hand moves to table. Top of tongue caresses point of upper left fang. Tongue moves to back of mouth. Probes lower surface of molars. Hand grasps coffee cup. Brings to mouth. Lips open. Swallow. Tongue licks upper left lip. Moves right. Body bends at waist. Left shoulder drops. Left leg draws fingers into skin below left ankle. Hand moves up outside of left leg. Hand moves to top of scalp. Fingernails repeatedly dig into scalp. Fingers caress scalp in circular motion. Scrape across temple. Move down left side of face to neck. Fingers dig into crevice of left collarbone. Fingertips wrap around bone. Neck muscles pull. Thumb bends and rests atop collarbone. Head tilts to left. Heat of fingers in collarbone crevice creates sweat. Right palm perspires. One by one, beginning with pinkie, fingers of right hand successively curl. Flat surface of each finger caresses palm. Fingers spring back in successive order. Fingers rub against one another. Sweat lubricates friction. Arm rests on chair arm. Lips form circle. Exhale on palm. Right hand in front of mouth. Lips expel. Hand grasps cup. Head tilts back. Lips open. Swallow. Swallow. Swallow. Swallow. Hand extends. Grasp with thumb and forefinger. Forefinger lifts. Arcs to opposite side. Fingers slide along gully where thumb meets index finger. Tip of index finger meets thumb in triangular formation. Left hand grasps. Flips. Left blade of hand moves away from body. Smoothes. Right hand rests on blade. Moves from wrist in half-spiral counterclockwise rotation. Hand moves slightly to right. Lifts. Hand rests on blade. Moves from wrist in half-spiral clockwise rotation. Hand moves slightly to right. Right hand rests on blade. Moves from wrist in half-spiral counterclockwise rotation. Hand slides right. Right hand rests on blade. Moves from wrist in full-spiral counterclockwise rotation. Hand moves to right. Drops. Hand moves back and forth. Reverses. Retraces movement in an inverted manner. Hand moves to right. Right hand rests on blade. Moves from wrist in full-spiral counterclockwise rotation. Hand moves to right. Hand moves to right. Drops. Hand moves back and forth. Reverses motion. Retraces movement in an inverted manner. Hand raises. Left hand slides away from body. Right hand drops. Right hand spirals counterclockwise. Lifts. Hand moves to right. Hand drops. Moves one hundred thirty-five degrees. Hand lifts. Moves upward ninety degrees. Descends two hundred twenty-five degrees. Hand moves to right. Pulls toward body one hundred eighty degrees. Hand doubles back two hundred seventy degrees. Turns right at ninety degrees. Hand moves slightly to right. Right hand rests on blade. Moves from wrist in half-spiral counterclockwise rotation. Hand raises. Moves slightly to right in half semi-circle. Stops. Repeats motion. Hand raises. Moves slightly to right.

13:00

Thumb screws. Wrist flicks two hundred seventy degrees. Right hand moves toward body one hundred eighty degrees. Hand moves in clockwise semi-circular direction. Fingers release. Hand rests, grasps and lifts. Lips open. Head tilts backward. Swallow. Swallow. Mouth floods with saliva. Tip of finger scratches outside of nose. Hand grabs. Elbow lifts. Elbow lowers. Elbow out. Body stretches. Thumb and four fingers grasp. Elbow raises. Hand drops. Motion reverses. Right hand grasps. Lifts. Lips open. Head tilts backwards. Swallow. Swallow. Hand drops. Rests. Body moves backward. Hands simultaneously grasp and pull down. Back slumps. Left hand grasps penis. Squeezes at base. Left finger squeezes. Blood rushes to head. Left hand strokes head of penis. Muscles contract in anal region. Hand releases. Penis falls to left side of body. Small movements in penis correspond to beating of heart. Left hand grabs base of penis. Displaces skin, moving from middle to top. Blood rushes to tip. Thumb lays across top as forefinger, middle finger, ring finger and pinkie grasp underside. Body pushes backward. Legs extend. Feet flatten. Hand massages head of penis. Repeat. Hand pulls skin over head of penis. Fingers release and dig toward anus. Fingers grasp. Quick successive stroking motions. Pubic area pulled in motion. Strokes on head. Hand releases. Body slouches then moves backward. Strokes repeatedly. Right hand moves to groin area and grasps testicles. Left hand continues to stroke penis. Middle finger of right hand probes anus. Stroke. Stroke. Stroke. Tip of middle finger inserts into anus. Left hand grabs and pulls breast. Successive strokes increase in speed. Testicles contract. Right hand probes testicles. Left bicep grinds. Breathing becomes stronger. Toes curl. Legs lift. Genital area sweats. Legs spread. Right middle finger presses anus. Left breast muscles pulse with arm movements. Profuse sweat appears on chest. Right hand massages belly repeatedly in circular counterclockwise motion. Left hand strokes penis. Pressure on bladder. Legs stretch out straight. Calf muscles tighten. Buttocks tighten. Sweat. Left hand continues to repeatedly stroke tip of penis. Right hand applies pressure to anus. Motion stops. Body slumps. Motion resumes. Body rocks back and forth. Knees move rhythmically. Buttocks and thighs jiggle in unison with stroking. Feet lift off ground. Toes point. Rapid succession of strokes. Left hand to mouth. Tongue touches left forefinger and middle finger. Thumb meets forefinger and middle finger. Fingertips rub counterclockwise. Left hand moves away from mouth and back to penis, stroking rapidly. Becomes faster. Calves tighten. Left hand to mouth. Tongue licks fingers. Hand returns to genitals. Hand grasps penis. Strokes. Facial muscles tighten. Body becomes rigid. Left hand to mouth. Lick. Hand to penis.

Sperm rises at base of penis. Testicles tighten. Stroking continues. Fluid appears at tip of penis. Anus tightens. Sperm spews from tip of penis over hands. Deep breaths. Legs slam. Hand tightens around penis. Successive waves of sperm emerge from penis. Legs stiffen. Stroking continues. Sperm cascades from tip of left-hand index finger onto back of left hand. Sperm flows onto thumb and into gully between thumb and forefinger. Blood rushes out of penis. Sperm dribbles out of penis tip. Body thrusts forward. Right hand clenches. Meets left. Fingers close. Left wrist moves back and forth. Body leans left. Left arm outstretches. Fingers flip. Right hand releases. Left hand grasps. Right hand grasps. Rubs across gully between thumb and forefinger. Right hand moves to top of head. Scratches. Right hand caresses left. Right hand on right thigh. Left hand grasps penis and squeezes from base causing sperm to flow from tip of penis. Right hand moves to tip of penis and dabs repeatedly. Left hand probes belly, pubic area and inside of thighs. Left hand grasps penis and squeezes. Sperm flows from tip of penis. Right hand dabs tip of penis. Left hand reaches. Fingertips flip. Right arm lurches backward then catapults forward. Fingers open. Exhale. Left hand to face. Fingers bend at knuckles. Thumb digs into crevice where left nostril meets face. Itches several times. Hands, in unison, grasp, pushing body forward. Right pinkie probes crack of anus.

Meat of palms thrust body. Rise. Walk. Left. Right. Left. Right. Left. Right. Left. Right. Left. Right. Body turns. Left. Right. Left. Right. Body halts. Arms drop to side. Right hand grasps base of penis. Urine streams from inside of stomach. Anus pushes. Bladder pushes ahead. Urine flows steadily from tip of penis. Urine alternately subsides and streams. Right hand shakes penis several times. Hand releases and crosses body. Arms stretch. Tip of finger presses down. Body turns one hundred eighty degrees. Walks. Left. Right. Left. Right. Left. Right. Left. Body halts. Sweat evaporates from pelvis. Body weight on back of right foot. Left foot on ground. Hips thrust right. Hand on right hip bone, forcing right elbow to bend ninety degrees. Buttocks tense. Knees straighten. Hips thrust. Buttocks slide to right. Body arcs. Mucus drawn from nose to back of throat. Swallow. Head leads body left. Left leg forward. Left step. Right step. Right hand on right hip. Step. Thighs and hip move in unison with steps. Hips sway left then right. Hips sway left. Hips sway right. Body turns left. Hand moves off thigh. Dangles at side. Walk. Left. Right. Left. Right. Left. Halt. Weight shifts to left side of body. Hand reaches. Grabs. Walk. Left. Right. Arm outstretched. Fingers close. Body turns. Walks left. Right. Left. Right. Arm grasps and moves in half-circle. Knees bend. Sit. Lean backward. Weight of body supported by rear of buttocks. Left hand grasps. Right hand grasps.

Arm cocks. Right arm moves up forty-five degrees. Hands move to genitals. Rub. Testicles relax. Left hand extends. Fingers open. Right hand grabs. Left hand grabs, forming tubular shape with fingers. Right hand lowers, pulling elbow into side of body. Left arm extends. Left hand contracts. Left hand grasps. Right hand moves to mouth. Lips open. Head tips back. Swallow. Right arm drops and releases. Right hand grabs. Lifts to mouth. Lips open. Head tips back. Swallow. Right arm drops. Hand releases. Feet propel body forward six inches. Left leg lifts. Crosses right. Thumb digs into right forefinger. Fingers move one hundred eighty degrees toward bottom of body. Repeats. Right hand grasps. Elbow extends into air and moves away from body forty-five degrees. Left hand grasps. Pulls toward body. Right hand crosses. Right hand moves left. Open. Glides across body. Fingers open. Close. Fingers form tubular formation. Right hand grasps. Thumb rubs back. Right hand releases. Elbow drops. Right hand grasps. Elbow lowers. Hand perpendicular to body. Right hand moves toward body. Sharply arcs in clockwise motion. Arm raises and moves toward mouth. Lips open and close. Teeth on right side close and open. Tongue moves to right side of mouth, pusing saliva to back of throat. Swallow. Elbow lowers. Hand perpendicular to body. Right hand grasps. Moves close to body. Sharply arcs away in clockwise manner. Arm raises and moves toward mouth. Lips open and close. Teeth open and close. Tongue scoops saliva from bottom of mouth. Teeth move in unison. Join. Separate. Tongue moves to back of throat. Swallow. Elbow lowers, perpendicular to body. Right hand to body. Sharply arcs away in clockwise manner. Arm raises and moves toward mouth. Lips open and close. Teeth open and close repeatedly. Tongue moves to right side of mouth. Push saliva to back of throat. Swallow. Fingers on right hand open. Left hand grasps, pulls, wipes. Right hand moves to mouth. Lips open. Front teeth close. Tongue moves to right side of mouth. Teeth meet. Peristalsis in trachea. Right tip of middle finger holds. Right hand moves to mouth. Lips open. Teeth rub on right side of mouth. Right hand grasps and moves toward mouth. Right hand touches lip on left. Rubs across center. Hands spread. Thumb and forefinger move to nose. Pinch. Inhale. Exhale through nose. Fingers move across bottom of nose. Right fingers grasp and rub left palm. Release. Left fingers grasp. Left fingers rub right palm. Wrist flicks. Right hand grasps. Left hand meets right. Both hands move toward mouth. Lips open. Hands rotate in unison toward body. Swallow. Swallow. Swallow. Left hand turns palm down. Moves right. Releases. Right hand grasps. Right hand moves to mouth. Right hand caresses lips. Left hand moves to head. Scratches. Right hand grasps using thumb, middle finger and index finger. Moves to thigh. Grasp. Lift. Thrust forward. Left hand probes anus then rubs thigh. Right hand moves toward mouth. Lips open. Swallow. Hands meet. Fingers intertwine. Thumbs stretch, barely touching one another. Head bows. Bridge of nose meets joined thumbs. Thumbs separate and apply pressure to sides of nose. Tips of thumbs rest on tear ducts. Right elbow flicks. Thumbs apply strong pressure to tear ducts. Thumb and forefinger grasp. Thumbs apply pressure. Breathe in. Breathe out. Arm extends. Thumb and forefinger grasp. Fingers separate by a centimeter. Thumb and forefinger push. Press. Fingers open. Thumb leads, forefinger follows. Flips. Gully between thumb and forefinger cradles. Hand drops. Wrist twists counterclockwise. Swift peck, up and down. Stroke toward body. Moves clockwise. Wrist twists counter-clockwise. Pecks. Moves right. Wrist twists clockwise. Moves right, parallel to chest. Hand moves two hundred twenty-five degrees toward left breast, parallel to chest. Strokes away from body forty-five degrees. Strokes toward body one hundred eighty degrees. Strokes parallel to body. Both hands lift. Left hand grasps. Right thumb drops. Hand lifts. Releases. Left index finger applies pressure. Arms stretch. Ribs thrust. Buttocks slide. Right hand grasps and moves to mouth. Left hand twists public hair clockwise. Lips open.

Hand tilts. Swallow. Right arm drops. Fingers open. Thumb and forefinger grind strands of public hair. Hair wraps around finger. Hair shuffles between fingers. Fingers move away from pubic area. Hands meet in front of body. Right hand grasps. Elbow up. Elbow down. Left hand grasps palm. Right hand grasps. Elbow up. Hand down. Head tilts to left. Grabs. Hand to mouth. Lips open. Head straightens. Lips moisten. Swallow. Left hand grasps and raises to face. Fingers rub mouth left to right. Rub side. Hand drops. Right hand grasps. Move to mouth. Lips part. Hand tilts. Swallow. Repeat. Eyes dart left to right. Ears twitch. Eyes look straight ahead. Focus. Double vision. Movement of mouth seen in periphery of vision. Eyes dart left. Big toe rubs toe next to it. Look straight ahead. Eyes gradually fall out of focus. Move left. Cast down. Left hand raises. Bends at elbow. Moves to left ear. Index finger extends. Rubs back of ear repeatedly. Right hand grasps. Lips open. Hand tilts. Swallow. Hand drops. Hand releases. Hands lay flat in front of body. Ears move slightly. Swallow. Right leg lifts, crossing over left. Press right calf muscle. Right hand moves to chin. Middle finger scratches chin several times. Head nods up and down in unison with finger. Hand drops. Eyes look left.

14:00

Deep breath in. Exhale. As air is expelled, chest falls. Shoulders protrude. Body thrusts forward. Palms of hands push down. Knees straighten. Buttocks raise. Body rises. Moves backward. Back of knees push. Body bends to left. Left hand grasps. Right hand grasps. Both hands thrust out from body. Fingers separate and pull. Body bends down. Slumps. Right foot raises. Bends at knee. Right foot hits ground. Left foot raises. Bends at knee. Left foot hits ground. Thumbs pull away from each other. Thumbs slip. Caress groin back and forth. Body leans forward. Bends at waist. Right hand reaches out. Left hand pushes down. Right finger scrapes body. Left hand grasps. Body turns. Walks. Left hand lifts. Body turns, reversing itself. Grasp. Right finger punches. Thumb and right forefinger pinch. Body arcs forward. Right forefinger hooks. Body reels back. Weight on left foot. Right foot lifts. Body leans. Grasps. Right hand pushes. Step. Step. Step. Right. Left. Right. Left. Right. Body turns left. Body turns right. Moves straight. Deep breath in. Left hand pulls. Right thumb nudges penis. Urine flows. Anus pushes. Bladder pushes. Anus contracts. Left hand shakes penis, flicking drops of urine. Lean forward. Left hand outstretched. Presses down. Body turns. Left. Right. Left. Right. Left. Right. Stop. Grasp. Arm muscles bulge. Moves forward. Right foot steps high. Bends at knee. Left foot drops. Ten tips of fingers push down.

Goosebumps appear all over body. Elbows on knees. Hands rest on chin. Eyes stare straight ahead. Forefingers push on eyelids. Red seen with streaks of green. Dots of many colors. Horizontal stripes appear in a field. Eyes ache from behind eyeballs. More pressure applied. Bluish ghostlike images of veins seen through closed eyelids. Eyes view retina and pupil. Press hard. Colors darken. Veins become white. Swirling red dots seen. Pain behind eyeball. Finger massages eyelids with great force. Hands cover eyes. Dots appear blue. Black field with bright blue veins. Sudden red shift. More light penetrates. Colored shapes appear, ending in center of pupil. Forefingers massage tear ducts. Blue seen. Repeated stroking of eyes. Field of vision goes dark. Throbbing pain behind eyeballs. Hands move away from eyes. Eyes close. Light turns vision olive green through closed eyes. Tongue licks upper lip, left to right. Mucus drawn from nose to back of throat. Mucus pushed to front of mouth by tongue. Mucus slides beneath tongue. Tongue reverses, probing area below. Tongue scoops mucus in its gully and divides pool of mucus into two. Mucus moves to back of tongue. Eyes open. Hand moves to side of face. Palms cover cheeks. Elbows crush knees. Back bends. Stomach breathes from belly. Mucus blocks air trying to pass through nostrils. Eyes dart left. Light forces eyes to move to right. Eyes focus closely. Glance afar. Register motion.

Dart downward right. Move to lower left center. Small motion attracts eye. Moves left to right. Focus upon lower right. Motion in peripheries. Eyes at rest. Lower-right-hand peripheral vision disturbed. Blink. Fills with water. Blink. Hand moves to eye. Rubs. Eyes open. Yawn. Belly rises and falls. Hands leave face. Move to thighs. Forefinger scratches skin beneath testicles. Hands clasp. Goosebumps appear over body then subside. Eyes cast downward. Glance upward. Look to left. Face ahead. Lean backwards. Weight on buttocks. Body reclines fifteen degrees. Right leg lifts. Extends. Straightens. Left leg lifts. Extends. Legs parallel. Toes on left foot separate. Right foot tilts. Calf flattens. Right calf bulges. Big toe flicks. Vein on top of right foot flicks back and forth. Toes on right foot wiggle. Muscles ripple on top of right foot. Eyes close. Middle finger moves to right thigh. Scratches repeatedly. Left hand moves to outer left thigh. Scratches repeatedly. Yawn. Hands outstretch. Clasp behind neck. Body moves backward. Neck thrust back. Toes wiggle. Eyes close. Swallow. Inhalation sucks gob of mucus from nasal passage to throat. Swallow. Mucus pushed to front of mouth on tip of tongue. Peristalsis slides mucus to back of throat. Left hand touches corner of mouth. Knees bend. Body slumps. Knees alternately straighten and bend. Legs push body back and forth. Hands clasp knees. Toes curl. Swallow. Look upwards. Eyebrows furl.

Tongue probes chancre sore on lower-left side of mouth below gums. Hand reaches into mouth and probes molar. Hand touches chancre. Hand leaves mouth. Clasp legs. Chancre throbs. Right thumb and forefinger scratch lower right earlobe in counterclockwise motion. Fingers grasp earlobe. Twists away from body. Tongue extends. Probes chancre. Pain drops into jaw. Tongue pushes against lower lip. Soft focus. Eyes double. Mucus drawn. Swallow. Swallow. Eyes cast downward. Swallow. Tongue emerges. Lick lips left to right. Left hand grasps right wrist behind thighs. Tips of feet stretch. Eyes move across body. Breathe from stomach. Back expands. Back contracts. Belly rises. Belly falls. Back thrusts forward. Drops. Close. Lips move. Eyes open. Swallow. Eyes close. Facial muscles relax. Back tingles. Chills emerge. Right hand moves to top of head. Fingernail scrapes scalp. Thumb meets each successive fingertip. Rubs. Thumb repeatedly flicks away from body. Goosebumps rise. Hairs stand on end. Waves of goosebumps cycle through body. Goosebumps recede. Continuous tingles. Swallow. Goosebumps rise on bottom of thighs. Eyes look down. View goosebumps. Toes tap. Left fingers draw chin. Repetitive horizontal scratching. Hand moves to nose. Left finger rubs outside of right nostril. Finger enters mouth. Tongue licks finger. Finger leaves mouth. Enters mouth. Finger probes interior of left nostril. Lubricated by mucus, finger slides counterclockwise. Finger moves from front of nose to back. Tip of finger probes inside ridge of nostril. Presses sinus. Protrudes from body. Finger enters right nostril. Digs counterclockwise. Fingernail plunges into dried caked mucus. Finger retreats from nose. Right index finger rubs against flat of thumb. Hand falls to thigh. Finger rubs thigh. Legs bend. Knees extend. Arms between thighs. Body erect. Left arm extends. Grasps. Walk. Right. Left. Right. Left. Body turns. Hand drops. Snaps. Urine flows in steady stream. Push belly and bladder and anus. Deep breath in. Stomach distends at lower abdomen. Anus relaxes. Releases gas. Left hand grasps penis. Shakes several times. Left arm extends. Fingers merge. Push down. Body turns one hundred eighty degrees. Walk left. Right. Left. Right. Hand slides over backside. Scratches. Left. Right. Left. Right hand grasps. Cradles. Bends. Rear end drops. Body drops. Left finger pushes. Legs cross. Thumb presses down. Thumb presses up. Thumb presses down. Moves to left. Right thumb presses out. Right hand, still grasping, moves to right ear. Mouth moves. Air glides across vocal cords. Step. Step. Step. Step. Hand grasps. Weight of body supported by right foot. Step. Step. Right. Left. Right. Left. Right hand raises to face. Rubs right eye. Step. Foot moves forward. Right foot supports weight of body. Left foot scrapes ground. Body weight on ball of left foot.

Back arches. Foot falls. Knees bend. Body weight shifts to left foot. Hand extends and grasps. Foot falls to right. Foot falls to left. Outside of foot falls. Foot flattens. Toe veins flatten. Muscles flex. Relax. Foot flattens. Widens. Heel down. Flat foot. Heel down. Flat foot. Heel down. Flat foot. Heel down. Flat foot. Right heel. Flat right foot. Left heel. Left flat foot. Left hand raises and grasps. Passes to right hand. Thumb, middle finger and forefinger hold body. Turn. Arm drops. Walk. Knees bend. Hands graze knees. Right elbow out. Knees straighten. Body turns. Left hand opens. Fingers extend. Right hand opens. Fingers extend. Right foot propels body. Slinks into crouching position. Weight on balls of feet. Arms outstretch. Right hand grasps. Left hand opens. Left hand receives. Right hand grabs. Left arm extends. Left hand opens. Left hand receives. Right hand grasps. Pushes. Right hand grasps. Body extends. Stretches. Turns. Right foot. Left foot. Pivot. Palm up. Hip thrusts out. Left hip pushes. Turns. Slinks down. Right hand grasps. Right hand grasps. Releases. Right hand grasps. Left foot shifts slightly toward right. Right leg saddles perpendicular to left foot. Left toenails dig into flesh of right leg. Move back and forth repeatedly. Right hand grasps. Body slides. Hand opens. Left hand grasps. Turns. Pushes away.

15:00

Left hand grasps. Right hand grasps. Left hand pulls. Releases. Left hand grabs. Right arm sweeps to right. Left hand reverses. Elbow out. Turns around. Right hand saws. Arm and elbow move toward body. Arm and elbow move away from body. Toward body. Away from body. Fingertips hold. In and out. In and out. Right hand releases and grabs. Left hand drops. Right hand brushes left fingertips. Left hand moves, turning entire body. Right arm extends. Right hand grasps. Right hand opens. Left hand closes. Body spins three hundred sixty degrees. Right hand grabs. Body bends. Left hand drops. Opens. Left hand reaches. Twists counterclockwise. Right finger slides across bottom of nose. Mucus coats upper surface of right finger. Left hand on left buttock. Right hand reaches. Twists clockwise. Body turns. Left arm extends. Left hand grasps. Right hand sweeps with blade. Body turns. Right hand grasps. Left hand grasps. Right hand grasps. Left hand grasps. Right hand grasps. Moves back and forth repeatedly. Left hand grasps. Slides. Elbow out. Elbow back. Elbow back. Body spins one hundred eighty degrees. Right hand sweeps. Right hand plunges. Right hand plunges. Right hand jingles. Shakes. Back and forth. Back and forth. Left hand grasps. Body spins. Left hand grasps. Moves to right. Body weight rocks back and forth. Shifts left to right. Quick motion. Left hand pushes. Thrusts. Right hand crunches. Right hand moves on top of left.

Fingers open. Left palm up. Left hand closes. Fingers clench. Right hand turns. Thumb and forefinger push away from body. Push away from body. Push away from body. Twist. Hand twists. Hand back. Tension in muscle. Hand moves. Muscles in hand tense. Left hand eliminates. Body turns one hundred eighty degrees. Pushes on top. Thumbs press. Fingers push. Press. Body shakes. Back and forth. Body shakes. Back and forth. Body shakes. Thumb pushes. Mouth opens. Lips lick. Hands lift. Plunge. Emerge. Immerse. Elbow out. Hands open. Grasp. Pull out. Emerge. Scoop. Shift. Scoop. Shift. Scoop. Scoop. Scoop. Left hand grabs. Both hands lift. Raise. Shake. Twist. Turn. Pull counterclockwise. Upend. Drop. Turn. Spin. Right arm spins clockwise. Elbow twists. Stops. Reverses. Meat of thumb quickly twists counterclockwise. Meat spins. Repeats. Spins faster. Hips sway counterclockwise. Stop. Tips of fingers grasp. Clockwise spins. Whole body shakes back and forth. Back and forth. Pelvis thrusts right. Releases. Arms outstretch. Raise. Arm tips parallel. Grasp. Pull. Right hand tears. Pats. Left hand smoothes. Left hand grasps. Right hand dumps. Body spins. Grasp. Right hand dumps. Right hand pinches. Turns. Right hand twists. Elbow moves toward body. Twists. Right hand twists. Elbow draws in. Right hand twists. Left hand grasps. Right hand twists. Right hand twists. Twists. Releases. Right hand trims. Left hand reaches. Wrist drops.

Left hand grabs. Steps right. Lifts. Lifts. Thumbnails dig. Water releases. Twists. Peels. Pokes. Releases. Pushes. Right hand crashes. Right arm raises. Repeats several times. Left hand twists. Pulls. Steps. Stops. Body spins to left. Walks right. Bends down. Scoops. Dumps. Digs. Drops. Walks. Right arm extends. Twists counterclockwise. Left. Right. Drops. Arm extends. Hands grasp and move across body. Hands immerse. Drops one. Drops two. Drops three. Drops four. Grasps. Middle, fore and ring finger rub against each other. In and out. Tongue smacks against palate. Grabs and wipes. Walks. Left. Right. Bends. Picks. Turns counterclockwise. Grasps. Rips. Left. Right. Two. Lifts. Turns. Elbows outstretch. Right. Drops. Up. Turns. Twists. Drops. Grasps. Slices in and out. One. Picks up. Back and forth. Two. Back and forth. Three. Drop. Turns right. Left. Grasps. Drops. Right hand shakes two three four five six. Twists counterclockwise. Dumps. Drops. Twists. Walks softly. Right. Moves in. Drops. Sit. Drops. Chews repeatedly. Shuttles left to right. Presses. Elbow drops. Deep inhalation. Chews right. Swallows. Stops. Clears throat. Breathes. Deep exhalation. Burps. Breathes in through nose. Stomach protrudes. Sides of stomach contract. Belly pushes out. Chest cavity collapses. Chest expands with breath. Out through nose. Shoulders raise. Sits. Legs spread. Hands in front, elbows on thighs. Teeth grasp thumbnail. Push. Push from center of stomach. Push.

48

Urine dribbles from tip of penis. Breathe steadily. Urine flows from tip of penis. Bowels open. Push from abdomen. Sphincter opens. Bowels fall. Push. Push. Urine trickles. Lips form words. Hands intertwine. Sphincter closes. Urine spews. Left hand reaches. Palms up. Both hands grasp. Pull toward body. One hand wraps over another. Stops. Pulls. Moves forward. Left hand moves between legs and rubs crack of buttocks. Sphincter loosens. Middle finger glides over anus. Pressure on coccyx. Arm reaches and grasps. Hand flattens. Twists back and forth. Hand moves between legs. Pressure on anus. Pulls. Drops. Hunches. Pulls. Lifts. Stands up. Drops. Turns. Hand reaches and pushes. Left hand grasps. Moves to right. Right hand twists counterclockwise. Right hand shakes. Left hand squeezes. Right hand surges. Quick strokes. Lips purse. Expel saliva. Quick strokes. Expel. Drops. Wipes. Moves left. Steps. Grasps. Both hands pull. Left leg lifts. Left leg drops. Right leg lifts. Right leg drops. Crouches down. Grasp two fingers. Flips. Stretches. Right leg passes. Left leg lifts. Body bends over. Snaps. Pull out. Grasps. Elbows out. Right leg opens. Up. Step through. Left leg lifts. Step through. Grasp. Pull out. Shoulders expand. Suck in. Stomach lifts. Pull. Grasp. Fidget. Fidget. Fidget. Pulls. Twist. Turn. Finger pulls. Tightens. Loops. Leg drops. Leg moves forward. Drops. Pull. Tightens. Loops. Hands move to knees. Step forward. Bend down.

Grasp. Grasp. Reach. Pulls down. Slide through. Shoulders hunch. Crimp. Pull out. Drop. Plug. Hear. Press. Right ear turns out. Grasps. Bends down. Pulls straight. Pulls tight. Grasp. Pulls. Step. Step. Stops. Inserts. Turns to right. Step. Step. Three. Four. Five. Step. Six. Seven. Eight. Nine. Step. Step. Eyes scan. Left hand pulls. Stop. Waits. Breathes. Again. Grasp. Step. Bend. Breathe in through nose. Steps. Vision shifts. Head nods. Rubs genitals. Pace quickens. Drop down over shoulder. Stop. Sit. Right leg crosses left. Dangles. Ankle moves up and back. Breathe from stomach. Left hand falls over. Tongue protrudes from mouth. Caresses upper lip moving from upper left to right. Tongue probes back of front teeth. Tongue chafes against sharpness of front tooth. Tongue moves to gums. Runs over crevice between two front teeth. Relaxes into slumped tongue. Probes bump on front tooth. Reaches up and grasps.

16:00

Feet draw. Knees bend. Shoulders arc. Ears tingle. Meat of palms wrap. Feet in. Out. Left foot withdraws. Bend at knees. Right foot extends. Right arm moves right. Left arm bends at elbow. Two hands push body. Prop. Slouch. Right thumb loops. Adjust chin. Right leg crosses left. Body supports palms. Shallow breath. Muscles tense around mouth. Upper lip strains. Tongue probes dry lower lip. Tongue moistens lips, upper then lower. Teeth grab lower lip and suck into mouth. Tip of tongue caresses lip. Teeth clench lower lip tightly. Skin stretches. Tongue licks lower lip. Tongue returns to inside of mouth. Moves to top. Left. Right. Body shifts. Leg lifts. Body slumps. Feet lift above pelvis. Right foot on top of left. Slide. Right hand on right buttock. Swallow. Breathe from stomach. Exhale through mouth. Back straddles. Right foot drops to parallel surface. Left foot parallels right foot. Knees at line of vision. Trunk and shoulders crunch head. Chin rests on chest. Buttock cheeks press together. Elbows support body. Coccyx lifts. Eyes pressured. Mucus drawn from back of throat. Legs spread fifteen to twenty degrees. Forty-five degrees. Feet, no longer parallel, mimic angle of legs thirty degrees. Feet mirror each other. Right foot slightly ahead of left. Index finger moves to bottom of nose and scratches four times. Hand resumes place next to buttock. Left hand clutches. Body slumps. Head rests. Inhale. Exhale. Pressure on back of head. Fingers dig into back of neck. Pain. Hand strokes hip. Repeat. Drop leg. Bend at knee. Finger enters nose. Quick movements. Pressure on neck. Left leg slightly bends. Right leg bends. Left leg spasms. Head shifts and wedges. Coccyx on edge. Right leg bends at severe angle. Hand rubs chest. Left hand dangles. Elbow joint fully extends. Fingers on left hand curl one at a time. Joints curl. Right finger moves across nose. Head readjusts. Left foot stomps. Heel slams. Toe. Heel. Toe. Heel. Toe. Teeth grind. Eyes lower. Shut. Breathing relaxes. Breathing steadies. Slight pressure on center of head. Finger moves underneath mouth. Right fingernail jams right gum. Fingernail jams harder. Digs under gum. Applies pressure. Eyes roll in back of head. Body props. Finger remains. Legs up. Right leg shifts. Finger probes upper right canine. Rubs against lower right canine. Swallow. Mucus retched from back of mouth. Arm raises. Right knuckles massage gum. Body swings. Hand adjusts. Sigh. Burp. Yawn. Yawn swallowed. Lick lips. Swing legs. Flip body. Walk. Lift head. Jam hands. Head turns slightly to right. Lift chin. Eyes scan. Yawn. Teeth clench. Arm lifts. Lick lips. Fingers slightly bend. Fingertips rest on palms. Tips of fingers move correspondingly to calluses on hand. Index finger rests on index callus. Middle finger rests on middle callus. Ring finger rests on ring callus. Pinkie finger rests on pinkie callus.

Pace quickens. Eyes look straight. Fist clenches. Thumb rests on index finger. Hand reaches back and twists. Pulls. Inserts. Scoops. Squeezes. Picks. Crosses. Clutches. Opens. Dumps. Closes. Forefingers loop. Slip back. Deep breath. Neck twists. Lower teeth grind against upper. Tongue pushes through top of teeth, extending one quarter inch outside mouth. Upper and lower jaw grip. Burp. Tug left arm. Wrist resists. Head turns slightly to right then back to center. Insides of thighs rub against one another. One foot steps in front of the other. Breathing corresponds every three steps. Exhale. Three steps. Arms swing back. Step forward. Left arm twists clockwise three times. Wraps. Moves. Heel hits. Toe. Lower and upper canine grab inside of cheek. Tongue caresses. Elbow swings. Hand drops. Left thumb meets forefinger. Snaps. Body turns right mid-step. Heavy step. Foot falls. Head turns. Pace quickens. One. Two. Three. Four. Five. Six. Seven. Eight. Nine. Ten. Eleven. Twelve. Thirteen. Fourteen. Fifteen. Sixteen. Seventeen. Eighteen. Nineteen. Twenty steps. Eyes adjust. Stop. Pull up. Hands flatten and slide. Thumbs out. Shallow breathing. Deep inhalation fills bottom of lungs with air. Exhale through nose. Head cranes to right. Back and forth. Forefinger rubs thumb, encircling thumb clockwise. Thumb traces. Arms extend. Joint releases from socket. Left arm detaches at shoulder. Body leans back. Proceeds forward.

Wrap. Breathe. Exhale. Right middle finger jabs. Left index finger pushes cuticle. Right ring finger peels cuticle. Stop. Start. Pressure wraps left hand. Right arm bounces against left hip. Left arm mirrors right. Bounces with hip movements. Right foot forward. Right arm back. Right middle finger rubs nose. Thumb massages pinkie. Swagger. Arms dangle at sides. Hand moves to shoulder. Hips sway. Buttocks sway. Right. Left. Right. Left. Right hand on right hip. Bones and muscles sway. Leg retreats. Buttock muscles extend. Leg forward. Buttock muscles withdraw. Bend down. Front thrusts. Torso moves vertically. Two fingernails dig into scalp. Nails push hair aside. Right middle finger moves to right thumb. Middle fingertip rests on right thumb meat. Fingernail digs into thumb meat. Skin indents. Fingernail leaves imprint on thumb meat. Middle finger springs away. Suck. Snort. Slide front. Spit gob. Right index finger bends. Finger moves to right edge of thumbnail. Springs back. Thumb bends. Meets ring finger. Ring fingernail digs into side of thumb. Fingers straighten. Thumb bends. Meets pinkie. Pinkie stretches. Meets thumb. Flesh of pinkie arcs to meet meat of thumb. Fingers separate. Stretch. Thumb twists perpendicularly. Thumbnail attempts to touch every nail on right hand. Right thumb extends. Touches nails beginning with pinkie and ending with forefinger. Fingers bend. Thumb straightens. Middle finger crosses and caresses cuticle of index finger. Fingers lay atop one another, rubbing repeatedly. Ring finger attempts to cross middle finger. Right pinkie attempts to cross cuticle of right ring finger. Pinkie shifts back. Three middle fingers on right hand join. Bend at middle. Overlap. Thumb bends. Pinkie attempts to cross three bent fingers to meet thumb. Fingers strain. Return to normal position. Arm drops. Grasp. Arm drops. Grasp. Right hand rests. Fingers bend. Fingers outstretch. Arc backwards. Fingers relax. Bend concavely. Right hand forms fist. Thumb bends. Settles perpendicularly across fore and middle fingers. Step up. Body weight rests on balls of feet. Deep breaths. Exhale. Tongue extends and touches cleft on lip. Right arm raises. Elbow juts. Wrist rubs mouth. Sucks mucus. Swallows. Butts tongue against forefingers. Chest swells. Right hand moves to nose. Scrapes away mucus. Hands fall to side. Fingertips swell. Right forefinger and thumb meet. Left forefinger and thumb meet. Together. Apart. Together. Apart. Fingers tuck. Together. Release. Together. Release. Together. Release. Tongue hangs out of mouth. Deep breath. Fingernail scratches upper part of ear. Index finger enters nose. Twists. Spits mucus. Pulls off balance. Drops hard. Nostrils flare. Pace quickens. Scratch. Lips purse. Push air. Facial muscles extend. Head turns right. Thumb hangs.

17:00

One. Two. Three. Four. Five. Six. Seven. Eight. Nine. Ten. Eleven. Twelve. Thirteen. Fourteen. Fifteen. Sixteen. Seventeen. Eighteen. Nineteen. Twenty. Hand digs. Extracts. Push. Insert. Close. Push. Step back. Step to side. Step forward. Step to side. Step forward. Dig. Drop. Step to side. Forward. Forward and forward pull. Push. Stop. Sit. Forward. Twist. Hand moves to mouth. Mouth opens. Swallow. Trachea drops. Straight. Cross. Left. Stop. Right. Push. Push down. Stop. Up. Hold down. Move down. Release. Reach. Swallow. Snort. Rise. Step. Right. Left. Step. Sit. Cross. Hands to face. Hands to ears. Muscles relax. Lips form. Elbows on knees. Pinkie over knuckle. Eyebrows furrow. Nose wrinkles. Eyebrows lift. Forehead ridges. Push down. Lips purse. Relax. Grasp. Push buttocks. Right hand flat against nose. Left hand caresses gully. Thumb and middle finger snap. Thumb meets forefinger. Attempts to flick. Legs cross. Elbows on knees. Fingers interlock. Small movements around mouth. Air passes through teeth and lips. Flows between teeth and inside walls of mouth. Eyes straight. Temples move from swallow. Left hand scratches length of right arm. Burp engages esophagus. Body spins. Stand up. Pull. Walk. Exhale. Swallow. Legs spread at point of connection to body. Back together. Feet touch one another. Legs angled thirty degrees. Arms mimic legs. Hands perpendicular. Thumbs move one sixteenth of an inch apart. Thumbs move one thirty-secondth of an inch apart. Thumbs move one sixty-fourth of an inch apart. Thumbs touch. Hands rest on belly. Heartbeat in belly. Inhale. Belly rises. Exhale. Belly drops. Left palm up. Right hand grasps right foot. Left hand grasps right foot. Foot pulled up facing face. Right hand lurks over side of foot. Toes intermingle with fingers. Arms outstretch, cradle foot. Pressure on elbow joints. Right foot and leg perpendicular to body and arm. Arms parallel. Fingertips tip in on tops of hands. Veins in right arm bulge. Elbow digs into right hip. Biceps flex. Foot against inside of forearm. Left hand grasps right forearm. Foot to face. Right big toe touches center of forehead. Tip of nose touches tip of foot. Release. Mouth closes around tip of big toe. Big toe enveloped by mouth. Big toe covered in saliva. Foot released. Stretch. Left hand grabs left foot. Right arm brings left foot to nose. Big toe of left foot touches tip of nose. Tip of foot rubs bottom of nose. Thigh muscles stretch. Foot shifts right, parallel to body, six inches from bellybutton. Three inches from bellybutton. Right hand grasps left foot and turns counterclockwise. Right meat of thumb meets ball of right foot. Right fingers grasp left toes. Wrap and stretch. Toes pull inward. Meat of right hand pushes right toes backward. Four toes bend perpendicular to foot. Right big toe twists ninety degrees to foot. Hands on chest. Eyes close. Yawn. Swallow.

Legs outstretch. Buttocks tighten. Weight of body evenly distributed between back of legs and buttocks. Light breathing. Eyes grow heavy and roll back in head. Eyelids three-quarters closed. Thumbs together, tips touching. Left hand on top of right. Scratch. Eyes close. Breathe deeply. Eyes open. Left hand moves to face. Index finger and thumb rub bottom of nose. Yawn. Ears click.

18:00

Reach. Grasp. Reach. Grab. Hold. Saw. Pull. Hold. Grab. Push. Itch. Push. Push. Turn. Walk. Two. Three. Four. Five. Six. Seven. Eight. Turn. Chew. Massage. Gather. Heavy. Slower. Reach. Open. Swallow. Exhale. Stand. Burp. Grab. Turn. Pick. Grab. Grab. Grab. Open. Turn. Walk. Pull. Grasp. Pull. Burn. Grab. Raise. Slump. Dig. Swirl. Cut. Peel. Chew. Swallow. Push. Stand. Move. Open. Grab. Close. Back. Forth. Left. Right. Grab. Push. Pull. Sit. Cross. Bring. Right. Chew. Swallow. Repeat. Dance. Reach. Push. Chew. Pick. Scratch. Stretch. Rub. Click. Peck. Hit. Shift. Roll. Pirouette. Push. Lift. Drop. Grab. Pull. Close. Grab. Stoop. Bend. Grasp. Pass. Open. Squeeze. Hold. Grab. Squeeze. Hold. Rub. Rub. Back. Forth. Hold. Turn. Pass. Pick. Backward. Forward. Twist. Turn. Flip. Shake. Unturn. Flip in. Twist. Bend. Drop. Grab. Rub. Squeeze. Shake. Flip. Lower. Lower. Lower. Round. Round. Drop. Pass. Flip. Tilt. Back. Forth. Forth. Back. Grasp. Pull. Pop. Twist. Pick. Drop. Through. Out. Down. Hold. Rub. Pucker. Tuck. Dump. In. Out. Stop. Sit. Bang. Lift. Insert. Bang. Hold. Slip. Lift. Spread. Insert. Pull. Tie. One. Two. Three. Four. Five. Six. Up. Stand. Step. Drop. Pull. Click. Pull. Blow. Walk. Pull. Turn. Turn. Straight. Extend. Slide. Stretch. Jostle. Steady. Twist. Extend. Exhale. Dart. Snort. Drop. Sit. Mumble. Quicken. Left. Right. Left. Cool. Walk. Gulp. Click. Smack. Draw. Loll. Dig. Itch. Shudder. Sip. Tip. Curl. Spit. Rest. Hear. Smack. Smack. Click. Lick. Inhale. Follow. Walk. One. Two.

One. Two. Reach. Scratch. Fidget. Pick. Burp. Bend. Up. Out. On. Blow. Wind. Bite. Cross. Scuttle. Twist. Turn. Bring. Tingle. Slide. Spit. Groove. Massage. Strike. Penetrate. Dig. Penetrate. Snort. Dig. Pass. Grab. Sigh. Lighten. Still. Pressure. Rush. Accentuate. Tuck. Raise. Gaze.

19:00

Refinger. Sneeze cross. Length of fore wipes free. Hand sad. Runs at bottom of thigh, no eye. Calflex. Peripheral movements spoken. Breath cools down right side. Jaws find teeth clenched. Outer part of lower fang, most pronounced grinding backward and forward. At course, cannot possibly reach gum. From which right fang descends. But nonetheless, it's a small rubbing. But chances are it's smaller. Lower gulch. Demanding attention from saliva. Mouth in general. Tongue dart. Clap. Knuckles twine thumbs. Nerves bounce up and down, up and down. In a vertical movement, movements are vertical. Few horizontals, particularly those of nervous origin. Protrudes taken. Teeth no longer relax. Teeth no touch. Palates separated. Naturally, overbite. Lower teeth tuck in front again. Never hitting gum, always hitting back. Teeth never touch except for teeth fall. Fall originates from gum. Does not happen. Protrudes in front of upper. Hip upper gum formation will not allow it. Conversely, from behind from in front. Still, nothing happens. Rasp hand. First now stretch. A knees. Burp. From deep within kiss from nose. Done back. To buttocks snap. At ease. Follows swallow. Somewhere between two palates. Not touching roof of mouth. And floating with teeth. Coming in. Which scratched by two. Thumb up in air like it. Return to lap. Right zero and left toe together. Inside shoe constrained. Taken and replaced. Come to face and adjust black.

Slips small makes noise held left hand. So forefinger joints of words. Peel sharp ridge. Forced and symmetrical and the late at noise. Let movements need its way. Flip silver flat side while held in place. Finger head and index finger. Light hand idle. Stroking on thumb. Lower fang meeting. Spinger thumb. Now is lift. Thumb to flip. Now thumb. Indents forefinger. Crease unnaturally lumpy. Right and right is face down on ground. Riched lightly. Arching four and blade middle and not touching ground. Still harrow. Body is sit. Licks wet. Whistle this time. Hey doe! Betsit. From chest: good girl! Good Girl! Happy to find highest. Slight pleasure gained from dig into finger and then pleasured by sharpness. Hoping to garner more pleasure through pain. But it ends. Foul smell knows. Non-neutral all day. Raised belt from lips. Head nod, yes, yes, yes, head nod, yes. Up and down. Up and down. Prince smile. Cheeks turn round and lift smile face. Too smile of day. Gray fly from middle finger. Macely in fact when last reported. Legs crossed. Hands pressed on warm ground. Back ground. Thigh to get slow blistering itch off hand. Ankle of new perfected above ground. Wallow tit clench drawn from nose. Palace of mouth. Insert back over ears. Below eyemaintainment. Tongue runs random. Pudding abounds sitting teeth inside gums. Back up over cloth spiny roof of the mouth. And super prongs curls back. Over the spiny, spiny doubles back like a folded forget that. Hung against tongue. Tastebuds massage tastebuds. Lubricated roof of mouth compelling three circuses. All at once spittle. Bottom. Bottom of bottom of bottom budside cannot go because it's black. Pothese stack. Death crumble when top of tongue presses upon them. Puffed out socks beneath tongue. Puffed when applied crumble into capillary-like berry. All held into place by extremely soft and moist is held is brink. Bind. Root in fact as in back as in bottom. Tongue finds right leg. As fine at very top straight piece of skin. Unpegged chip of tongue. Stealing very hard ridge. Very hard skin in its septemberary. And it runs as very far as it can back to the back. Cast open wide an order for such a thing to happen. Tongue begins capade. Licks wrist. Teeth exposed as smile yeah. Deep wave of spax. Side of insulated socks exists as second chancre sore. Hoo hoo arises. Giggle hits head. So, tongue could not find the mace. Inside I think feels warm. Overruns tender. As young I'm sorry, as tongue. Skatial tightens. Folds scaling part. And tips and tops. Tears of moment at which scaly part ends intermediary area. Soft pon ridges. And thereto finds another puffy sac. Whoa puffy sac. View tongue can't quite reach. Cold nervous to touch the puffy top, with puffy sac and top. Puffy six times over closing. Goose meat perhaps heaven on surface. Rush bone on metal grate. Index finger rubbing bits wallow.

Seem to suck and vacuum and laser on palate where all is gathered and sucked down off toes and swallowed. Ratia invisible stomach, where nothing is felt, where nothing is perceived. Lift lips lick – start again – tongue lifts lick tongue lifts lick. Nap around three times. Stone is back into mouth. Merges on face. That scene picturely in bottom of mouth. Words deformed easily as craw earlier in synchronicity. List not hand and facial muscles. Root together in a non manner. Wallow. Thrills now around toes. On round at thirty-degree angle thirty-degree angle low bathed. Shed between bottom of calm and buttocks. Locks against right outer right foot turn. Overlooks down chords. Crap and crust areas between thighs. Though eyes make lines aware. Cords on their own have no attention. Or on crack area. Crack area at rest. Low swung at rest. Quench simultaneously quench. Unsafe skittish thought. Deep breath leaving loose nation of hands. Here's what happens to you: white thumb drifts into pocket. In sync thirst of wallet. Vile of face. Mouth fraught. Teethy ware of smile. Line entry. Thumb nothing. Between mouth and mind. Last blinking. Swallow hole. Tears annoying with head asleep in sound. Nottom hitting. Bladder presses palm from drink. A nation of dividends. Recast a while away. Right ruckus itch. Saliva's snout. Pressure pressure to keep thumb at bay. Terror is left by all knuckles in lap hand. Hands move to maker.

Hands white on hands help in pocket. Rocket bottle down. Lips wrap with half a goes ridges. Pagan swallow little effort. Little word little remains in front of mouth. Liquid elevator tongue. Going up on little place. Nerves feeling pressure from liquid again. Listlessly from back. Clenched hands move into throat. Be brow and periphery. Gondize liquid. Headless down, headless self. Bladder falls.

20:00

Whitehead and watch after left hand. In the pocket worthwhile by all pass flat on ground lifting body. Horror body weight on foot. What put blade outward. Holting ground. Toe hitting leftly. First hat off ground, dancing about hand and knee. Lift head reference. Thandclaspsle. Extend out in sled. Brokenicular clap in scent of body. In the chive leash forward. Stay stay, no. Rightut. Arched egg. Feet and egg platforms. I mean then a platformed body as does leave somewhat unsteadily. Buttocks slime. Food all the way. Food now bearing equal weight of body. Shit I suppose now kisses the balls skeet. Grab by stomach facing up. Arms are let down. Pace resumes those mucusy. All pockets are respect, who is knocked down? Finally found in right bass. Sinease right good. Still suspicious as draft walking has begun. Loose breath is taken and death is through nose. Seems suspicious in digs below. Hand by hand. Issue is replace. Drink the paper. And the wine. Forcing skull arms and fingers goat indictment. Grasp button through guides button through. Stamp in pockets. And arc climb and blather. It's able to be with read hung. Not stretch lips lip. Rccnd. Refeel. Feel the first feel. Of the ground. Feet of pockets. Feels opening unsuccessful. Warm larm. Crack of new cover. Would that full on arms. Mind is taken. And in pockets taken. Eyes read truth forty one. Eyes stand island. To the bagger. So berkenrodgers el.

Greens projectile. On ah squint. Elen crows on tongue. With muriss. Kush jimmyhands. Cinder hung moistened. Soldiers stable. Midgets in palm. The latter affair. Lowerslime. Your pinch yearning. When again when again when again. Gas zippers why. Hung moves overflip. At last light da da oop. I'm famous steel. Drow. Breath from beast. Saliva molar palate polster up. And flexor. And raid to hire the public loop. Home of the thieves and it's gone. Odd blue veins and strange dips of flesh. Anchor beauty in mirror. White and largest but odd can never see mirror. Stock bloat. Draw on a convulsion ounce. And that crazy rear on a string. The mouth open, white. Oh and it's much more complicated than tongues can ever feel. Showling spittle. Slower than loose that creates language. The body external feast of language. To what to eye. Across thumb through right heart. Leanstrongly. What traday. White and white no one would think. Mucus dances white. To fiddle play twist. And capped white middle finger. Fear on the right side eyebrow. Forefinger macabre. Mistare fear. Thank you someodd hour. Accentuating rough skin. Bind thighs. Mask of the swallows tightens. Lipsmart. Deep spittle save a one. Near incident. Knees paralyzed. And it's a hundred percent head pulp. Slinks on left hand foot. Eyeing top of eyebrows. Distend over eyes. Knock since unblemished by time. Unblemished lincoln smileon. Mature coverge. Meat eyes.

Tufts deep in flesh bolds. Stethdescend forcing ventral eyebrow. Stipped for fourth time. Right nip unhand across lip. At eight twenty-five eye damage custard. And silence is guide. Lips fall down, except on pavement. Body only river. Second body is gone to river. Over probablestone. A plash. Deepin. That's right. Always strange feet. Soaked inhale. We'vot stealth dodder pinched. Thumb places craft mmmm. A tan reaches out. Linky hung deformed gully. Whistle without lips. Get hum. Sunset eroticism breedy. Walk nine all night. Slowing down I quit time. Assidiously affaxed on face. Clap lunge being longly. Grouping folds around right lay hard pullie. Spitting marin. Right thumb nubs right thumb. Backwards I walk through nuance. Push the body move. Backwards right. Right foot backwards behind luck. Body bends collar. Achivment hair. More the upmean liquid. Walk backward from joint. Hay subs spouting saliva. Ripe darkening oval in arm. Rotter movement. Flexivly flexivly. Swallow black and white. Breakfast taken as eyes in upper thigh spot. And here last mind see moon. Head reigns pollows upper right. And eddy many more looks. Sahn eyes scanning. Out through mind flips. Chills emerge over to the right. New stun wooing me to the giving forget the eyes. And the eyes from whence I came. Eyes right hudson. Teeth swallow. Runny eyesight joggles side of face. Fun eyes nine.

At nides, head tilts. Body smile permanently. Clap meated fist meated fist. Right arm fooled spermly. Body pulled beef. Right thumb in egg. Eye walk with no eyes. Arm distracted from joint. Suds spouting saliva. Darkening bones. Fixed on pivoting tip of back. Flexity flexity spring rack. Eyes swung hairdo. Cling clay claw. Deafens heights. Hung a mean left sole. Head preeing into hudson colors. Pray eye gone out viewing. Up body. Up spine. Through shoulders lack lack pork. Overturehum old eyes yes. Runny eyes wallow. Flatter vein again. Leftwards dug index. Wallo bit of palm. Bleeds exploding in ears. Cheap grind projectile. Chippity tongue flip. So long arm.

21:00

eleven hours walking body moves arm swinging contraunison leg movements deep breath inside salivation nine pm left finger index finger rubs eye counterclockwise one two three times tip of finger moist from eye fluids deep breath mucus expulsion via spit deep breath yawn eyes view sky getting darker upper teeth bite outside of lower lip little finger of right hand itches above eyebrows walking fingers curl on right hand particularly pinkie nestled in flesh of palm thumbs leads out burp left leg crosses over right walk left right left right moon rises deep breath might fist moving in out one two three four he no he right hand reaches into back pocket knees bend in tripod five after nine licks lips licks lick tongue licks lips this monday nite stop deep breath look to left eyes see new building index fingers curl up hand falling off waist exhale walk walking forward right hand grasps drops eyes cast downward face breaks into smile body turns left walk straight down nose pulls mucus yawn cover mouth by right hand right hand falls to side of body smile body stoops down right hand points and snaps presses down left hand finger inhale hands on knees back bends snap hand raises salutation right hand raises salutation breath exhale east sky dark teeth upper teeth outside mouth on top of lower lip upper lip combs mustache of lower lip lower lip right hand wipes fallen mucus from nose deep breath in full breath out tongue moves to back of upper cheek back of upper front teeth back and forth horizontally deep breath breathe out nose arm extends from body wraps clockwise straight on one foot in front of other left arm cranks face from walking steps left and right and left and right and left and right and left and right left and right down two steps right hand pushes right hand digs left hand plugs and turns right hand grasps stairway and railway and banister one two down one two one two turn left right left right turn upstairs heart pumps on top of right banister deep breath in deep breath out tongue on tips of lips deep breath elbow jams body turns to left door shuts drop thumb and forefinger of left hand reach and grab pass to right and drop grabbed by left hand reaches two drops folds between two hands drops right hand extends out pulls moves straight left hand switches right hand pulls down left hand opens up right hand penis urine flows sigh left hand touches head of penis right hand supports left reach and flips counterclockwise urine swallows buttocks squeeze buttocks push out abdomen pushes out breath out squeezes abdomen and buttocks right hand grabs penis clutches shakes left hand pushes down wipes left hand right hand grabs throws into left hand left hand right hand scrubs left hand left hand scrubs right hand body lowers right hand scrubs left hand left scrubs right right foot kicks kick off left right hand turns both hands join face body bends at waist walk right hand shuts left right left right walk left hand digs gathers body turns to right drops body finds right hand sits down opens right hand pulls flips around right hand sits describes counterclockwise one swooping down towards body six with counterclockwise six points described as counterclockwise seven two three three written one in angle counterclockwise line draw interior and six counterclockwise point one seven horizontal to body dot seven nine counterclockwise seven composed of three strokes and of three left hand fingers hold and grasp right hand takes and fits licks lips lips lick left hand twists and right hand flips left knuckles right hand below left knuckles arms straight out deep breath as eyes close room slightly spins clockwise forty-five degrees straight line deep breath into belly deep breath out mouth head rises hand grasps thumb pushes boom boom middle finger right hand eyes upward right middle finger moves left pinkie pops right foot tucks under chair foot hold bar of chair from left in between left big toe and left index toe through sock hugging chair left hand reaches out left hand to forehead right hand massages left temple finger moves lower left hand right hand presses horizontally hand moves forward stop pressed by right finger left finger moves to upper left hand down and to right left hand releases right hand releases finger left hand right index finger moves down release right forefinger and left thumb together left nail digs into right forefinger teeth clench left foot runs along left edge left hand moves from forehead and right finger hits left finger hits right finger hits left finger hits right finger hits right pinkie hits breath enter enter enter breath body turns left walk forward left hand clicks grabs with left hand forefinger digs in deep one two with right hand left hand pulls open tongue licks lips from left to right bends down right hand grabs left grabs walk right hand opens right hand extends grabs moves left right hand grabs clenches one two three four five seven ten eleven thirteen turns hand grabs dumps right hand twists and leans up and stretches right hand opens left hand extracts right hand holds left hand opens crushes between right middle finger and left thumb right hand opens left hand closes right hand grabs shakes three times walks over drops right hand grabs tongue and massages left hand grabs transfers to right hand left hand grabs stops dumps right hand grabs finger digs deep digs right finger hand unscrews left forefinger digs in drops breath left hand grabs right hand screws counterclockwise right hand digs finger with left hand drops into right hand flicks three times and grabs counterclockwise stirs right hand grabs left elbow tips up out from body right hand grabs left hand holds right hand twists several times clockwise left hand replaces weight of body shifts to left foot right hand grabs eyes search upward left hand opens hands pull up over waist right hand digs in left hand grabs left hand holds right hand returns right hand stirs clockwise right hand drops right hand holds left hand extracts left hand pulls down right hand grabs and chops one two down right elbow out hitting body right hand gathers and throws body backs back right hand turns counterclockwise stirs right hand grabs brings to lips swallow left hand turns right hand grabs right hand tilts right hand grabs nine fifty one right hand grabs chops mashes all weight on left hand right thumbnail picks and drops right hand scores one two three four five six seven eight nine ten times gathers left hand feeds to right body moves and drops turns drops walks two three four five six deep breath inhale hands rub left hand grabs right hand grabs right arm moves out right arm and left arm in unison move up and down left hand turns right hand grabs and passes to left right hand grabs elbow out right hand turns two three four five six seven eight times right hand grabs right hand grabs dumps left hand grabs moves out right hand grabs body grabs arms of chair move in at crease of legs and turn forward left hand moves out right hand gathers legs thrust body up

22:00

.etarapes regniferof dna bmuht thgiR .flac thgir sehctarcs
dnah thgiR. .ydob dniheb tsiF .regnif elddim thgir fo pit yb
del ,swercskroc dnah thgiR. .sllup wolbE .esir skcottuB
.nethgiarts seenK .thgir petsediS .tnorf ni sevom mrA .snepo
dnah tfeL .tnorf sehcniP .petS .drawkcab teeF .tfel snruT .ydob
morf sevom dnaH .esolc sregniF .ydob ot sevom dnah tfeL
.petS .petS .petS .petS .petS .spets toof thgiR .taorht fo kcab
morf dehsup sucuM .sdnetxe toof thgiR .nethgiarts seenK
.llab yb deL .sesir leeH .drawkcab petS .dnuorg stih toof thgiR
.tfel stfihs thgieW .sllaf toof tfeL .leeh no thgieW .stih llab
thgiR .petS .petS .llab ta sdnE .leeh ta snigeB .spets toof tfeL
.swollof toof tfeL .tfel sgniws toof thgiR .tfel snrut ydoB
.dniheb seyE .stfil toof tfeL .dneb seenK .deb stih gel tfeL
.thgiew ydob stroppus toof thgiR .dnuorg ffo stfil leeh thgiR
.revo sdneB .osrot morf sdneB .ydob sdneb dnah tfeL .sdneb
kcaB .ydob sleporp gel tfeL .sesiar toof fo llaB .drawkcab
seenK .tfil eot eiknip ,eot htruof ,eot driht ,eot dnoceS .spord
eot gib fo piT .roolf morf stfiL .stcartnoc toof thgiR .deb fo
egde morf sevom eenk thgiR .snettalF .snethgiartS .tfel spilF
.elpmet ta stratS .egacbir reppu ta sdne hctertS .tcartnoc seenK
.nwaY .elkna separcs gel tfeL.sesir ylleB .sllaf ylleB .sesir ylleB
.levan morf sllaf ylleB .sesir ylleB .sllaf ylleB .sesir ylleB
.tcartnoc sgnuL .seitpme ylleB .slliF .gel ni doolB .hgiht tfel ni
ssenllitS .deb ffo stfil gel tfeL .taorht morf dehsup sucuM

84

.dnuorg ffo stfil eenk fo edis thgiR .gel tfel fo sriah sehsurb
leeh thgiR .eenk thgir fo edisrednu morf evom seot tfeL
.snethgiarts gel tfeL .scra kcaB .snethgiarts gel thgiR .wollip
otni sknis daeH .tfel ot thgir pil reppu skcil eugnoT .avilas
sdiovA .ecaf morf sevom dnah tfeL .staerter sivleP .sesneT
.stcartnoc gel tfeL .sneffits osroT .nwaY .nwod seyE .thgir seyE
.eson eliforp seyE .pu seyE .tfel seyE .xaler selcsum daeheroF
.pord sworbeyE .esolC .tfel ot eson eliforp seyE .snepO
.wodahs yb decnahne noisiV .thgir ot eliforp eson sweiV
.snepO .elgnis esoN .nepo seyE .eson seyE .wollaws fo o
dnuor smrofed htuoM .spil seyE .wollawS .sdneB .snethgiartS
.llits gel tfeL .sehcrA .deb morf sevom eenk thgiR .snethgiartS
.trapa seenK .stcatnoc mra tfeL .daeh fo tnorf ni evom sdnaH
.snethgiarts gel tfeL .selgnaD .spord gel thgiR .nwaY .elahnI
.stcartnoc hcamotS .stcartnoC .stsurht sivleP .snettalf kcaB
.daeh tnorf ni kcolnu smrA .sepiW .lirtson ot sucum dekac
sdda regniF .lirtson tfel fo epahs ot mrofnoc ton seod regnif
fo epahS.regnif fo epahs ot mrofnoc ton seod lirtson tfel fo
epahS .lirtson edisni segdir sdiova regnif fo piT .sevaeL
.lirtson morf sevom regniferoF .stfil dnaH .snethgiarts woblE
.nwaY .stcartnoc mrA .skcottub otni dna xyccoc htaeneb
sedilg regniF .pitregnif yb deilppa erusserp thgilS .suna dna
skcottub fo kcarc morf sedecer regnif xednI .llits slianregniF
.skcottub morf stfiL .kcab morf sevoM .spord dnaH

.snesool elpmet tfeL .reppu morf etarapes hteet mottoB

.stsurht sivleP .snepo waJ .xaler hteeT .nettalf seoT .nethgiarts

seenK .hctertS .nwaY .edis no ydoB .hctertS .sgel neewteb

sdnaH .stsurhT .eye tfel yawa sevom regnif elddiM .worbeye

tfel segassam regnif xednI .eye sbur eikniP .ecaf morf sevom

dnah thgiR .sucum sretslob avilas yretaW .wollawS .hteet

morf yawa eugnot sehsup riA .elahxE .nesool selcsum kceN

.wollawS .lrucnU .avilas kciht secudorp eugnoT .swollawS

.htuom fo tnorf ot hsuP .hteet fo wor pot sesnaelc eugnoT

.keehc thgir fo hcuop morf slepsiD .htuom fo tnorf sdoolF

.taorht morf eson ot dehsup sucuM .snethgiarts wolbE .rae

thgir morf straped dnah tfeL .tfel spilf ydob san nethgiarts

seenK .seenk morf sevom mra thgiR .noitisop latef morf

sdnapxe ydoB .enilriah ot worbeye morf sevom regniF .semit

ruof sehctI .daeherof ot enilriah morf sevom regnif xedni

thgiR .warD .elahnI .lirtson srevocnu bmuht thgiR .eson morf

sevom dnah thgiR .wollawS .sucum dna avilas slepsid eugnoT

.eson otni taorht fo kcab morf dehsuP .tcartnoc skcottub tfel

dna hgiht thgir ni selcsuM .deb morf stfil eenk thgiR

.stcartnoc pih thgiR .sdrawkcab ydob sleper toof thgiR .stsiwt

dnah thgiR .ehtaerB .bmuht fo roiretni sesserac regniferoF

.esolc sregniF .stcartnoc wolbE .elahnI .lirtson thgir morf

sevom regnif xednI .sepiW .sesrepsid sucuM .daerps

regniferof dna bmuhT .pil no sucum sdragersiD .sgnul ot

nward eson morf riA .esolc sregniF .daerpS .eson morf sevom

woblE .snepo dnah thgiR .stcartnoc gel tfeL .deb morf sesir

eenk thgiR .deb morf sesir eenk tfeL .tfel stsurht sivleP .seenk

ta nethgiarts sgeL .ni smrA .stcartnoc redluohS .lruf sregniF

.stcartnoc smrA .sliart sbmuhT .spit sessim riaH .daeh fo edis

diova sregnif fo spiT .srae revocnU .swaj morf evom sdnaH

.gnirps sbmuhT .kcen esaeler sregniF .spord woblE .waj morf

yawa hsup sdnah fo sleeH .kcen morf evom sdnah fo kcaB

.lruf sdnaH .kcen fo edis morf evom selkcunK .stsurht woble

thgiR .redluohs thgir morf sevom tsiF .selkcunk sbur bmuhT

.snepo dnah thgiR .drawnwod snrut woblE .kcen sdiova tsiF

.specib morf sevom bmuhT. .redluohs morf sevom bmuhT

.snethgiarts woblE .nepO. esaeler sregnireroF .sexaler bmuhT

.swercskroc mlaP .htuom fo tuo sedils eugnoT .hteet hguorht

gnissap ,htuom fo roiretni sretne eugnoT .gniliec morf yawa

woble stsurht tsiwt esiwkcolcretnuoC .sdneb mrA .daeh fo

kcab morf yawa wollip sehsurb mra thgir thgiartS .spord

daeH .wollawS .tcartnoC .dnirG .xaler swaJ .wollawS .pil fo

cra gniwollof tfel ot htuom fo edis thgir morf gnivom pil

reppu ssorca snur eugnoT Eyelids close.

AFTERWORD

'Vocable Scriptsigns':
Differential Poetics in Kenneth Goldsmith's *Fidget*

Marjorie Perloff

Eyelids open. Tongue runs across upper lip moving
from left side of mouth to right following arc of lip.
Swallow. Jaws clench. Grind. Stretch. Swallow. Head
lifts. Bent right arm brushes pillow into back of
head. Arm straightens. Counterclockwise twist
thrusts elbow toward ceiling. Tongue leaves interior
of mouth passing through teeth. Tongue slides back
into mouth. Palm corkscrews. Thumb stretches.[1]

It reads at first like a section from a Beckett prose text: the late
All Strange Away, for instance, with its graphic account of the
movements made by an unspecified figure, confined in a
small rotunda:

Head wedged against wall at a with blank face on left
cheek and the rest the only way that arse wedged
against wall at c and knees wedged against wall ab a
few inches from face and feet wedged against wall
bc a few inches from arse, puckered tip of left breast
no real image but maintain for the moment, left
hand most clear and womanly lightly clasping right
shoulder ball ...[2]

But *Fidget*, as Kenneth Goldsmith has titled his recent verbal/
visual experiment, is not literary invention but *poésie verité*,

a documentary record of how it actually is when a person wakes up on a given morning. If, in one sense, it recalls Beckett, it is also written under the sign of the photographer Edward Muybridge. As Goldsmith explains:

> Fidget's premise was to record every move my body made on June 16, 1997 (Bloomsday). I attached a microphone to my body and spoke every movement from 10:00 AM, when I woke up, to 11:00 PM, when I went to sleep. I was alone all day in my apartment and didn't answer the phone, go on errands, etc. I just observed my body and spoke. From the outset the piece was a total work of fiction. As I sit here writing this letter, my body is making thousands of movements; I am only able to observe one at a time. It's impossible to describe every move my body made on a given day. Among the rules for Fidget was that I would never use the first-person 'I' to describe movements. Thus every move was an observation of a body in space, not my body in a space. There was to be no editorializing, no psychology, no emotion — just a body detached from a mind.[3]

Telling the 'truth', Goldsmith quickly discovers, may be the biggest 'fiction' of all, it being humanly impossible to track all of one's bodily movements. At this very moment, I am moving my fingers over the computer keyboard as I type, flexing my left foot, wiggling my left toes and running my tongue over my upper lip from right to left. As I note those movements, I am making others that go unrecorded.

Indeed, as Goldsmith admits, after five hours of the experiment in which he monitors his body as it gets out of bed and interacts with objects like coffee cups, he 'began to go crazy'. The exercise becomes harder and harder, the verbal equivalents to physical motion more and more abbreviated. By 6:00 PM, 'as a defense my body put itself to sleep'. When Goldsmith awakes and realizes he had another five or six hours to go, he panics:

> I went out and bought a fifth of Jack Daniels, walked over to an abandoned loading dock by the West Side highway and drank the entire bottle, all the while continuing my exercise. Needless to say, I got trashed. I found my home and fell asleep by 11:00 PM, never once having stopped my narrative.

Later, when he plays the tapes, Goldsmith finds that in the drunk sequence, his words have become completely slurred and in the last chapter (22:00), quite incomprehensible. So, in a Beckettian move, 'I ran the first chapter backwards, mirrored it, then reversed every letter.' For example, 'Tongue runs across lower lip, moving from right side of mouth to the left following arc of lip', becomes

> .pil fo cra gniwollof tfel ot htuom fo edis thgir morf gnivom pil rewol ssorca snur eugnoT.

The sentences from this last chapter were then put into reverse order with the last actions coming first, and the first coming last.[4] The only exception is the very last line of the book, 'Eyelids close', which is printed in standard order, 'creating a full circle of closure for the day'. And further: the tapes were then rigorously edited: all unnecessary words such as 'the' were removed as were all possible literary and art references. The aim was to make the text 'very dry and very descriptive' and 'to divorce the action from the surroundings, narrative, and attendant morality'.

These statements must be taken with a grain of salt. For one thing, the 'closure' provided by the final sentence of the thirteenth chapter, 'Eyelids close', is called into question by the various versions in which Fidget exists. The piece, which exists as a plain text version[5], was given a gallery installation at Printed Matter[6], a performance at the Whitney Museum of American Art at Philip Morris (16 June 1998)[7], and a 'fidgetty' Java Applet website, made in collaboration with programmer Clem Paulsen[8]. But more important: the ostensibly 'dry' and 'descriptive' report of successive body motions quickly takes on an air of surreality as the artist poses the question of what it would mean to be aware of every physical motion one makes. The more empirical and detailed the verbal transcript, the more absurd the attempt to 'translate' body motion begins to seem. Faced with a welter of ceaseless and simultaneous movements, the mind censors out about 99% of these movements and subjects the rest to increasing interpretation. The 'factual' account thus becomes more and more idiosyncratic, and what Fidget celebrates with perverse charm is the victory of mind over matter, and the inability to convey what we call body language except through language. The text is thus a devastating send-up of the now all-pervasive

Foucault-inspired discourse on bodily primacy, a discourse that, in the wake of Elaine Scarry's famed *The Body in Pain*, generates such book titles as *Apocalyptic Bodies, The Body in Parts, Leaky Bodies and Boundaries* and *Performing the Body*.⁹

Consider, for example, the narrator's account in chapter 2 (11:00) of going to the bathroom and urinating:

> Walks. Left foot. Head raises. Walk. Forward. Forward. Forward. Bend at knees. Forward. Right foot. Left foot. Right foot. Stop. Left hand tucks at pubic area. Extracts testicles and penis using thumb and forefinger. Left hand grasps penis. Pelvis pushes on bladder, releasing urine. Stream emerges from within buttocks. Stomach and buttocks push outward. Stream of urine increases. Buttocks push. Sphincter tightens. Buttocks tighten. Thumb and forefinger shake penis. Thumb pulls. Left hand reaches. Tip of forefinger and index finger extend to grasp as body sways to left. Feet pigeon-toed. Move to left. Hand raises to hairline and pushes hair. Arm raises above head. Four fingers comb hair away from hairline toward back of head. Eyes see face. Mouth moves. Small bits of saliva cling to inside of lips. Swallow. Lips form words. (*Fidget* 14-15)

Why is this description of the most ordinary and trivial of human acts so unsettling? Whereas a satirist like Swift, in 'A Voyage to Brobdingnag', reveals the inherent hideousness of the human body by means of gigantism ('[The nurse's Breast]

94

stood prominent six Foot and could not be less than sixteen in Circumference. The Nipple was about half the Bigness of my Head, and the Hue both of that and the Dug so varified with Spots, Pimples and Freckles, that nothing could appear more nauseous')[10], Goldsmith is determined to keep his eye, so to speak, on the ball, to record noncommittally and nonjudgmentally the way the body actually works. And yet that very 'objectivity' has the Swiftian effect of demonstrating the stark disconnect between the physical and the mental, between the rote performance of the bodily function and the human ability to 'form words'. As the 'eyes see face' in the mirror, the implicit question seems to be Hamlet's: 'Is man no more than this?'

In breaking down bodily functions into their smallest components, Goldsmith defamiliarizes the everyday in ways that recall such Wittgensteinian questions as 'Why can't the right hand give the left hand money?' In ordinary discourse we take a verb like 'walk' for granted, without dwelling on the fact that 'walk' means to alternate the forward motion of right foot and left foot. When we refer to a man urinating, we don't usually note that the steam of urine 'emerges from within buttocks'. And when we say someone 'speaks', we don't bother to add that 'Mouth moves' or that 'Lips form words.' 'Four fingers comb hair away from hairline toward back of head': it couldn't be a more common gesture but the standard reference would be 'to push the hair out of one's face'. The near-rhyming locution 'four fingers comb hair ... from' takes a moment to recognize for what it is. And when in chapter 3 (12:00), Goldsmith has his morning cup of coffee, the ritual becomes more elaborate than a ballet number or an athletic contest:

> Back on back of chair. Legs touch legs. Arms parallel arms of chair. Hands grasp end of arms. Legs push back. Feet flat on ground. Elbow on arm. Arms out. Cup to mouth. Swallow. Cup put down. Teeth outside mouth. Legs lift. Legs stretch on legs ninety degrees. Grasp paper towels. Slide to front. Left hand grasps right. Pull away from left. Left hand stretches. Fold. (Fidget 22)

The relation of human arms and legs to the metaphoric arms and legs of a chair, the place of the teeth as one opens one's mouth wide enough to drink, the movement one makes when folding a paper towel – all these take on an aura of gravity as if something of great importance is taking place, something in need of urgent commentary.

But of course such self-consciousness, or more properly body consciousness cannot be sustained and so the entries get shorter and shorter and by the time we get to chapter 9 (18:00), we read the following:

> Reach. Grasp. Reach. Grab. Hold. Saw. Pull. Hold. Grab. Push. Itch. Push. Push. Turn. Walk. Two. Three. Four. Five. Six. Seven. Eight. Turn. Chew. Massage. Gather. Heavy. Slower. Reach. Open. Swallow. Exhale. Stand. Burp. Grab. Turn. Pick. Grab. Grab. Grab. Open. (Fidget 62)

Mostly monosyllabic verbs without subjects or objects, often distinguished by a single letter as in 'Grasp'/'Grab', and permutating through the chapter which ends with the rhyme 'Raise. Gaze.' In the next chapter (19:00), drinking has begun and all hell breaks loose. The objective reporter now gives way to the inventor of language play:

> Refinger. Sneeze cross. Length of fore wipes free. Hand sad. Runs at bottom of thigh, no eye. Calflex. Peripheral movements spoken. Breath cools down right side. Jaws find teeth clenched. Outer part of lower fang, most pronounced grinding backward and forward. (Fidget 66)

And on the next page:

> Spinger thumb. Now is lift. Thumb to flip. Now thumb. Indents forefinger. Crease unnaturally lumpy. Right and right is face down on ground. Riched lightly. Arching four and blade middle and not touching ground. Still harrow. Body is sit. Licks wet. (Fidget 67)

The more the language of description breaks down into non-sense and neologism, the greater, ironically enough, the need to make value judgments. The hand is now unaccountably 'sad', the 'eye' missing, the 'crease' (between fingers?) 'unnaturally lumpy'. One cannot, it seems, remain detached from one's body, from one's own reactions. 'Slight pleasure gained from dig into finger and then pleasured by sharpness', remarks the narrator (*Fidget* 67), now wanting to put his stamp on events as they occur. The language becomes his language and the next chapter (20:00) opens with the sentence 'Whitehead and watch after left hand', where the first word in initial (and hence capitalized) position, refers not only to a whitehead or mole found on the left hand, but to the philosopher Alfred North Whitehead, whose famous Fallacy of Misplaced Concreteness (e.g. if a tree falls in the forest when no one is there to hear it fall, does it make a sound?) is apropos to Goldsmith's narrative. The poet further puns on 'watch', which looks ahead to the phrase 'In the pocket worthwhile' in the next sentence. And the creation of a new language field leads to the finale with its reversal of words, giving us new entities like '.petS .drawkcab teeF' (Feet backward. Step). The reversed linear flow makes a key word of 'morf' (from), a word highly applicable in the context along with 'woble' (elbow), 'pil' (lip), and the mysterious 'evom' (move), which looks like a number or symbol in a Cabbalistic game. The morfing landscape is full of 'sredluohs' (shoulders), 'eugnot' (tongue) and there is much 'dna' (and) about. It seems, finally, that the language game has occluded the multiform activities of the moving body. And so 'Eyelids close'.

Here, then, in Beckett's words about *Finnegans Wake*, 'form is content, content is form. [The] writing is not *about* something; it is that something itself.'[11] But the paradox – & this is a new development in poetics at the turn of the twenty-first century – the written text is only one of *Fidget*'s realizations. Earlier, I mentioned the Whitney installation, the musical performance score and the Java applet. Let me now say a further word about this latter electronic version, which reconfigures the text of *Fidget* by substituting the computer for the human body. As Goldsmith explains:

> The Java applet contains the text reduced further
> into its constituent elements, a word or a phrase. The
> relationships between these elements is structured
> by a dynamic mapping system that is organized
> visually and spatially instead of grammatically. In
> addition, the Java applet invokes duration and
> presence. Each time the applet is downloaded it
> begins at the same time as set in the user's computer
> and every mouse click or drag that the user initiates
> is reflected in the visual mapping system. The
> different hours are represented in differing font
> sizes, background colors and degree of 'fidgetness',
> however, these parameters may be altered by the
> user. The sense of time is reinforced by the
> diminishing contrast and eventual fading away of
> each phrase as each second passes. [12]

Time is speeded up in the applet so that each hour period takes approximately five to seven minutes to complete. The viewing of the Java applet from any specific site would take about eighty minutes, and then the cycle begins all over again. No one, of course, is likely to sit at the screen for the full cycle, but even a few minutes of access reveal some interesting facets of *Fidget*. When the text's linear momentum is replaced by spatial organization, words interact in new ways. Thus, in the case of the opening sequence ('Eyelids open. Tongue runs cross upper lip. ... Grind. Stretch. Swallow'), in the electronic version 'swallow' appears center stage and rests on top of 'Tongue runs across upper lip'; it is then replaced by 'grind' and 'stretch', the words grinding against one another and causing a kind of traffic jam as the screen fills up with what looks like a spiderweb of action verbs connected by lines that appear straight, then bend and stretch. But in the visual mapping system, verbs like 'bend', 'clench' and 'swallow', detached from their subject and object nouns, and given relatively equal weight, become less referential, less narrative and – oddly – less male-oriented. In its book version, Fidget is quite obviously a man's narrative, especially in the masturbation passage in the fourth chapter (13:00). But in the applet, words appear as words rather than as signifiers of X or Y, morphology and physical appearance taking precedence over denotations. In the 15:00 chapter, for example, the opening sentences 'Left hand grasps. Right hand grasps' are transformed into overprint, intersecting and coming apart on the yellow 15:00 background, marking their symbiosis as do 'lifts' and 'lips', and those 'elbows' appear, replace one another and disappear in what looks like a balletic structure. As a visual and kinetic space, Fidget has an austere and silent beauty quite different from the printed version or from its oral enactment, for, as seen on the screen, this language has neither memory nor agency. Indeed, the elegance of the clean, undifferentiated visual space suggests that, as the poet Tan Lin put it, 'the mind is only vestigially connected to the body "it speaks" through'.[13]

And yet – and here is a further irony – the training ground for producing this electronic text, I would argue, may be found in Goldsmith's earlier, and by no means 'elegant' written work, *No.* III 2.7.93-10.20.96 – his encyclopedic poem based on words ending in the sound *ah* (*schwa* according to phoneticians), a collection of words drawn from conversations, books, phone calls, radio shows, newspapers, television and especially the Internet, that was arranged alphabetically and by syllable count (from single-syllable words beginning with A – 'A, a, aar, aas, aer, agh, ah, air' – to D. H. Lawrence's complete 'The Rocking Horse Winner') so as to create a Gargantuan poetic reference book or archive on the *argot* of our times[14]. The sensitivity to language displayed in *No.* III, a text still subject to conscious arrangement rather than indiscriminate recording as in *Fidget*, clears the ground for the onscreen paragrammatic possibilities we now witness in Goldsmith's work.

'If literature is defined as the exploration and exercise of tolerable linguistic deviance', write Jed Rasula and Steve McCaffery in the introduction to their new anthology *Imagining Language*, 'the institutional custodianship of literature serves mainly to protect the literary work from language, shielding it from the disruptive force of linguistic slippage'.[15] Such slippage has increasingly become a poetic norm, creating a new poetics we might call *differential*. For Goldsmith's text is not 'intermedia' in the usual sense (e.g. word + image or word set to music or recited on film) but a work that has been produced differentially in alternate media, as if to say that knowledge is now available through different channels and by different means.

Indeed, one of the great pleasures of *Fidget* is that its differential mode allows for an unusual degree of reader/listener/viewer participation: it is the reader, after all, who must decide whether to access the 20:00 chapter of *Fidget*, in which case s/he cannot 'read' the other twelve chapters, or whether to 'read' linearly by moving from page to page of the written text. Reading – looking – listening – surfing: this is a work that gives engagement a whole new dimension.

Notes

1 Kenneth Goldsmith, *Fidget* (Toronto: Coach House Books, 2000). All further references are to this edition. Selections from *Fidget*, which covers the day's first three hours, was published in a limited edition of 100 copies, signed and numbered, on the occasion of the Whitney Museum of American Art at Philip Morris commission between Theo Bleckmann and Kenneth Goldsmith and in conjunction with exhibitions at Printed Matter, Inc. by Stadium Projects, New York, NY. See also the internet version available at www.chbooks.com/online/fidget/index.html. The website includes the Real Audio files from Theo Bleckmann's vocal-visual interpretation, as presented at the Whitney Museum of American Art on Bloomsday 1998, the complete text of Fidget in thirteen chapters from 10:00 to 22:00, and a Java applet version.

2 Samuel Beckett, *All Strange Away in Rockaby and other Short Pieces* (New York: Grove Press, 1981), pp 58-59.

3 Goldsmith, letter to the author, 9 October 1998.

4 This seems to be a direct allusion to Beckett's *Watt*, Chapter III, in which Watt, unable to cope with 'reality', begins to invert, first the words in a given sentence and then 'the letters in the word together with that of words in the sentence together with that of the sentences in the period', as in (spelled phonetically) 'Dis yb dis, nem owt. Yad la, tin fo trap' (*part of night, all day. Two men, side by side*). See Beckett, *Watt* (New York: Grove Press, 1959), p 168. I discuss Beckett's reversals here in *Wittgenstein's*

Ladder: Poetic Language and the Strangeness of the Ordinary (Chicago: University of Chicago Press, 1996), pp 139-40.

5   The Whitney edition will soon be available from Coach House Books, whose online site is www.chbooks.com.

6   The gallery installation, according to Goldsmith (letter to the author, 9 October 1998) consisted of 'twelve paper suits (one for each hour of the day). Each suit had the entire hour of the day printed on it. Following the trajectory of the day, the earlier suits were printed with very light text and the suits later in the day were printed in reverse, with white letters on black paper. Also, following the emotional/psychological trajectory of the day, as my mental state grew shakier, so the text on the suits grew less legible and more smeary (this was achieved with a Xerox machine).'

7   In performance at the Whitney Museum of American Art (June 16, 1998), Theo Bleckmann, the lead singer for Meredith Monk, 'stood high on a balcony in the museum and dropped sheets of paper printed with each word as he sang them. These sheets of paper were picked up by a pair of twin children and brought to a team of seamstresses, who sewed them into a suit during the course of the hour-long performance. When Bleckmann had finished singing, the then-finished suit was hoisted up to his balcony, where he donned the language/actions that he had just spoken/sung. Hence, a full circle was created' (letter to the author, 9 Oct. 1998). In an article for *Poliester* (Fall 1998), Bill Arning, who attended the performance, reports: 'To hear the expulsion of morning mucus from the nostrils ethereally sung

by Bleckmann was as startlingly incongruous as to read such an unsensational act described by Goldsmith as if it were a recipe for a difficult but exquisite souffle.' For further discussion of the Bleckmann performance ('a cross between a Gregorian chant and a medieval Book of Hours'), see Nancy Princenthal, 'Artist's Book Beat', *Art on Paper* (November/December 1998): 70-71.

8   The site may be accessed on www.chbooks.com/online/fidget/index.html.

9   I take these titles at random from the most recent Routledge book catalogue (1998/99): Tina Pippin, *Apocalyptic Bodies: The Biblical End of the World in Text and Image*; David Hillman and Carla Mazzio (eds.), *The Body in Parts: Fantasies of Corporeality in Early Modern Europe*; Margrit Shildrick, *Leaky Bodies and Boundaries: Feminism, Postmodernism and (Bio)ethics*; and Amelia Jones and Andrew Stephenson (eds.), *Performing the Body: Performing the Text*.

10 Jonathan Swift, *Gulliver's Travels*, in *The Writings of Jonathan Swift* (New York: W. W. Norton, Norton Critical Edition, 1973), p 71.

11 Samuel Beckett, 'Dante ... Bruno . Vico .. Joyce,' *Our Exagmination Round his Factification for Incamination of Work in Progress* (Paris: Shakespeare and Company, 1929); rpt. in Beckett, *Disjecta: Miscellaneous Writings and a Dramatic Fragment*, ed. Ruby Cohn (New York: Grove Press, 1984), p 27.

12 See www.chbooks.com/online/fidget/about.html.

13 Tan Lin, 'Information Archives, the De-Materialization of Language, and Kenneth Goldsmith's *Fidget* and *No. III* 2.7.93-10.20.96', Art Byte, Feb-March 1999, as posted on Goldsmith's web page, http://wings.buffalo.edu/epc/authors/goldsmith/lin.html, p 1.

14 In a letter to the author of 14 March 1997, Goldsmith explains his technique in *No. III* as follows:

> I was inspired by the explanation given to me regarding the sacred significance of the Sanskrit word *aum*. It seems that when one speaks this word, all parts of the mouth are engaged ... My function for the next 3 years was that of a collector of language ... I would carry around a portable dictaphone and a notepad and whenever I would encounter one of these [*ah*] sounds, I would 'capture' it. At first, my idea was to take all sounds regardless of their content .. perhaps, I thought, with this system I could subvert the normal function of language (communication) and invoke a less conventional idea (although not without precedent) of language as pure music. And language is a great medium to do this with because no matter how much one collects for sound alone, there is *always* meaning.

Goldsmith's arbitrary limits (600 pages of material gathered between 2.7.93 and 10.20.96 and arrangement via the alphabet and syllable count, gives us such bravura passages as the following sequence of three-syllable units beginning with *wa* (see No. III 2/7.93 –10.20.96, Great Barrington:The Figures, 1997), p 27: Wadada, waheena, wahoodler, waiting for, wallflower, wallpaper, walls have ears, WankStoppers, Ward Cleaver, warm moisture, warmaster, warrior, Warszawa, wassailer, wasted years, watch out for, watch the wear, wave-lover, wayfarer, Wayfarers.

15 Jed Rasula and Steve McCaffery, *Imagining Language: An Anthology* (Cambridge and London: MIT Press, 1998), p x.

Thanks to:

Theo Bleckmann for his inspired vocal treatment of Fidget, Debra Singer and the Whitney Museum of American Art at Philip Morris for commissioning and presenting Fidget, David Platzker and Printed Matter, Ron Wakkary and Phil McConnell of Stadium Projects, and to Clem Paulsen for his hours of sweaty genius in programming the Fidget applet. Also, thanks to Vivian Selbo, A.G. Rosen, Sydney Maresca and Andrea Scott for their efforts toward making Fidget a reality.

Typeset in Joanna and Gill Sans and printed at Coach House
Printing on bpNichol Lane, 2000.

Edited and designed by Darren Wershler-Henry

To read the online version of this text and other titles from
Coach House Books, visit our website:

www.chbooks.com

To add your name to our e-mailing list, write:

mail@chbooks.com

Toll-free:

1 800 367 6360

Conventional mail:

Coach House Books
401 Huron (rear) on bpNichol Lane
Toronto, Ontario
M5S 2G5